ACCIDENTS IN NORTH AMERICAN MOUNTAINEERING

VOLUME 9 • NUMBER 5 • ISSUE 63
2010

THE AMERICAN ALPINE CLUB
GOLDEN, CO

THE ALPINE CLUB OF CANADA
BANFF, ALBERTA

ISSN: 0065-082X
ISBN: 978-1-933056-25-8
ISBN: (e-book) 978-1-933056-26-5

Manufactured in the United States

Published by:
The American Alpine Club
710 Tenth Street, Suite 100
Golden, CO 80401
www.americanalpineclub.org

Cover Illustrations
Front: Mike Isom, the victim of an ice climbing fall in Little Cottonwood Canyon on December 31, 2009, being raised by a Lifeflight helicopter. Photograph by Rick Egan. (See report under Utah.)

Back: Titcomb Basin, Wind River Mountains, Wyoming. After breaking trail for 21 miles over three days during a spring attempt of Gannett Peak, our anticipated weather window dissolved with the swift arrival of another storm. After using up our "storm days" waiting for a clearing, we made one summit attempt but were denied by the continuing storm. Our retreat was equally as harrowing, accentuated by poor visibility, explosive winds, and numbing cold. Without our navigation information, experience with the terrain, and proper equipment, we would have been in serious trouble. Fortunately, we got out with good memories and good friendships. Photograph and comments by Matthew Jesperson.

CONTENTS

ACCIDENTS IN
NORTH AMERICAN MOUNTAINEERING
Sixty-Third Annual Report of the American Alpine Club

This is the sixty-third issue of *Accidents in North American Mountaineering.*

Canada: Canada submitted narratives for 2009, but no data for Tables.

United States: *Errata: First, Last year's cover page incorrectly indicated the Volume as being #10. It should read #9. We bind four to six Numbers, depending upon total number of pages. This makes up one volume. Second, a fatality was reported from Colorado's Eldorado Canyon. The source was Boulder's* The Daily Camera. *The report of his demise, as Mr. Twain would have said, was premature. He is indeed alive.*

It was another year of rappel and lowering errors. Several of them appear in the narratives. The usual causes—rope too short and no knot in the end(s) of the rope(s)—were indicated. An interesting new one was the result of using a rope too small in diameter for the device being used—a Grigri. And in another case, an individual threaded his lowering rope through a webbing anchor sling at the top. The resulting friction caused the rope to burn through it. It is hard understand why we are still seeing these errors when so much basic information is to be found in "how to" books, catalogues, on the Web, and at frequently visited climbing sites.

Two citations came to our attention this year. One involved a woman from Lithuania on Mount McKinley. She demanded to be flown out—even going so far as to call her embassy on a satellite phone from the mountain—despite her injury being very minor and manageable. The other citation was given to a group of hikers who used a SPOT device to call for a rescue from the Grand Canyon. The park determined this helicopter evacuation to be a false alarm. When the party was asked what they would have done without the SPOT device, the leader stated, "We would have never attempted this hike."

There are some very moving first-person narratives that were sent forward. (See California especially.) The details and facts found in these incidents are greatly enhanced by the authors' personal observations and feelings expressed.

There are still a number of climbing areas not reporting data or incident reports, including such popular areas as Joshua Tree National Park (CA) and Baraboo State Park (WI). On one blog site, there was a complaint that we do not seem to report any incidents from any of the many local crags in Massachusetts. It's time to point out once again that we are only as good as

a) the managers of public and private lands and b) the network of volunteers who are willing to participate in contributing to this effort.

As mentioned in previous issues and throughout this report, there are some web-based resources that often provide good information and accident stories. Here is a short-list of some of those sites:

http://home.nps.gov/applications/morningreport/
www.supertopo.com
www.mountainproject.com
http://www.tuckerman.org/
http://www.mountrainierclimbing.blogspot.com/
http://www.friendsofyosar.org/

In addition to the dedicated individuals on the Safety Advisory Council (especially Aram Attarian, who is now taking on Colorado and the Southeast), we are grateful to the following—with apologies for any omissions —for collecting data and for helping with the report: Hank Alacandri, Erik Hansen, Janet Miller, Leo Paik, Justin Preisendorfer, all individuals who sent in personal stories, and, of course, George Sainsbury.

John E. (Jed) Williamson
Managing Editor
7 River Ridge Road
Hanover, NH 03755

jedwmsn@mac.com

Rob Davidson
Canadian Editor
Alpine Club of Canada
Indian Flats Rd
Canmore, AB T1W 2W8

anameditor@alpineclubofcanada.ca

CANADA

FALL ON ICE – PLACED NO PROTECTION, INEXPERIENCE
Alberta, Canadian Rockies, Waterton National Park

On January 1, a group of climbers met at a popular ice climbing area in Waterton National Park. Upon arriving at the base of the climbs, it was discovered that another party had begun up the easier of the climbs, French Kiss. Of the group, only one felt confident enough to lead the harder climb, Quick & Dirty. The climber moved slowly and appeared to be having trouble placing an ice screw near the top where his protection was dangerously run-out. He eventually fell a distance that landed him within a few metres of the bottom of the climb. It is estimated that the distance was between 40 and 50 feet. The climber landed upside down with the screw he was trying to place in one hand and one axe in the other. His helmet was cracked on one side. Miraculously, he suffered no immediate injuries, but was still taken to emergency services and monitored thereafter. (Notes: The biggest fall any of us had witnessed—including rock climbing. The climber was using double ropes. The one that held the fall was retired. The ice screw held the fall. It was retired due to the magnitude of the fall, even though there was no observable damage. The Yates screamer that was attached to the screw fully deployed.)

Analysis

In hindsight, as the climber proceeded up the climb it was noticed that he moved slowly. He placed protection earlier than normal off the start of the route and neglected to place protection on an easier ramp before the final crux, leaving him dangerously run-out by the time he was tired. The climber was the youngest of the group (early 20s) and visiting from Quebec. He claimed to be quite involved with ice climbing there. Even though he displayed initial confidence in leading the climb, the older and more experienced climbers (who knew they were not in shape to lead it) should have acted on the warning signs earlier. They could have at least suggested he place a screw at the ramp before heading up to the crux. The climber could have retreated long before realizing he was in trouble. (Source: Aaron Davydiuk, climbing party member)

FALL ON ROCK – HANDHOLD CAME LOOSE
Alberta, Kananaskis Country, Mount Yamnuska

On May 23, a climber had a leader fall approximately 140 metres up the route Bottleneck (5.8, seven pitches) on Mount Yamnuska. The leader sustained a broken ankle. The party was unable to self-rescue or descend further. They

3

waited on a ledge 125 metres below the summit for Kananaskis Country Public Safety Specialists. A top-down rope rescue was completed with a Public Safety Specialist being lowered from the top at 1816, reaching the climber at 1836, administering first aid, and then being lowered to the base at 1933. The total length of the lower was 270 metres.

Analysis

A handhold broke and the climber barn-doored off the face. He was caught by his belayer, but hit his foot on a small ledge in descent. (Source: M. Koppang, G. Field, B. Duncan, Kananaskis Country Public Safety Program) *(Canadian Editor's Note: Whenever possible, parties should attempt to complete a self-rescue.*

There were a total of 18 submitted accidents in Kananaskis Country for 2009. Several of the accidents involved hikers or scramblers in technical terrain, including one fatal fall.)

FALL ON ROCK – FOOTHOLD BROKE OFF, OFF ROUTE, PLACED NO PROTECTION

Alberta, Canadian Rockies, Phantom Tower

On April 11, a party of three were going to attempt the South Face of the Phantom Tower, a 5.8 gear route in the Ghost River. The leader (20) started up what he thought was the beginning pitch, but he was about 20m too far to the right. He ascended about ten meters from the ground without protection. A foothold broke off, and that resulted in a ground fall and a long tumble through the scree. His partners secured him with the rope and then activated the "911" button on their SPOT beacon. The Banff detachment of the Royal Canadian Mountain Police (RCMP) were eventually contacted by the SPOT dispatch, and they phoned Banff Public Safety dispatch to inform them that there was a PLB 911 signal coming from the east side of BNP. The RCMP had to place a call back to the International Emergency Response Coordination Centre (IERCC), in Houston, Texas, as they had not provided latitude and longitude with the initial call. RCMP called back with the coordinate, and the location was determined to be on the BNP east boundary, near Phantom Crag.

Meanwhile, a caller from the party eventually made it through to Banff dispatch on a cellphone, and confirmed that a 20-year-old male had fallen ten meters to the ground and had sustained serious injuries. Parks rescuers and EMS flew to the scene and heli-slung into the patient, who was then stabilized, packaged and slung down to a heli staging area. STARS air ambulance was notified and they flew directly to the scene. The patient was then transferred directly to Foothills Hospital in Calgary, where he was diagnosed with fractured vertebrae.

Analysis

SPOT beacons are becoming very popular. Unfortunately the details of the incident and sometimes the actual latitude and longitude of the incident are not properly communicated. This makes mounting an appropriate rescue response more difficult. Often the text message on the beacon has not been updated for the trip and is not appropriate. Placing no protection at the beginning of the climb guarantees that any fall will result in hitting the group and significantly increasing the potential for a serious injury. (Source: Brad White, Banff National Park Mountain Safety Specialist)

ROCK LEDGE BROKE OFF — FALLING ROCK HIT CLIMBING PARTNER
Alberta, Kananaskis Country, Mount Yamnuska

On May 22, JK and A were climbing the Necromancer route (5.10a, eleven pitches) on Mount Yamnuska. JK was leading the second pitch and stepped on a ledge to start a traverse when the ledge broke off. A soccer ball-sized rock landed on A's foot breaking it. JK lowered off gear, tandem rappelled with A off the route, and splinted the foot and leg once at the base. A was heli-slung from the base by Kananaskis Country Public Safety Specialists. (Source: Kananaskis Country Public Safety Program)
(Canadian Editor's Note: Loose hand and footholds are not uncommon in the Canadian Rockies. This is a good example of the party being able to self-rescue and administer first aid while waiting for an organized evacuation.)

FALL ON ROCK, INADEQUATE COMMUNICATION, INADEQUATE BELAY — BELAYER NOT READY
Alberta, Canadian Rockies, Wicked Gravity Wall

On June 16, PH was sport climbing on the Wicked Gravity Wall at the Back of the Lake climbing area at Lake Louise, Banff National Park. He had done several routes and was climbing one last route to "cool down" before dark after a long afternoon/evening. After feeding the rope through the station, he neglected to inform his belayer that he was ready to be lowered and he just leaned back. The belayer was not holding the rope at the time and PH fell about 20-30 feet, striking a ledge with his feet on the way down. Eventually the Grigri belay device stopped him just before a ground fall, but he suffered a badly broken ankle. Rescuers responded in the dark and PH was lowered in a stretcher over the steep terrain and then wheeled to the ambulance in a stretcher.

FALL ON ROCK, OFF ROUTE, PROTECTION PULLED
Alberta, Kananaskis Country, Mount Yamnuska

On June 18, W and NB were climbing Grillmair's Chimney (5.6, 8 pitches) on Mount Yamnuska. W was leading and went off-route. NB lowered W on a single piton, which pulled free. W fell approximately eight metres, resulting in a compound fracture to the left ankle. NB splinted the ankle with an ice axe and then rappelled the route, ran down the trailhead, and then borrowed a cellphone to call 911. Kananaskis Country Public Safety Specialists responded where the injured climber was heli-slung off the route.

Analysis

W could not reach a bolt, and therefore in desperation placed a piton to be lowered on. The piton was not fully placed, and thus pulled. (Source: M. Koppang, G. Field, B. Duncan, Kananaskis Country Public Safety Program)

FALL ON ROCK – PROTECTION PULLED
Alberta, Kananaskis Country, Mount Indefatigable

On July 1, KT and MH were climbing the rock route Joy (5.5, 10 pitches) on Mount Indefatigable. KT was leading and built an anchor and was ready to belay MH. KT tested the anchor, which pulled out, then KT cart wheeled off the ledge and the back-up point pulled free. KT fell past MH, who held the fall. KT's helmet came off during the fall and he hit a ledge on the way down. KT came to rest hanging upside down and bleeding heavily. MH was able to call out for help. Nearby hikers contacted the Kananaskis Country emergency dispatcher. Kananaskis Country Public Safety Specialists heli-slung KT off the route where he was transferred to an air ambulance. (Source: Kananaskis Country Public Safety Program)

ROCKFALL FROM PARTY ABOVE, POOR POSITION
Alberta, Canadian Rockies, Abbott's Pass

On July 6, JPL was approaching Abbot's Pass hut from the Lake O'Hara side when a party above kicked off a very large loose rock (approximately 1.5 metres by one metre). The rock luckily split in half just before hitting JPL in the back and smashing his face into the rocks. An UIAGM mountain guide who witnessed the incident called for help and assisted JPL up to the hut where rescuers landed with the helicopter and took JPL to the ambulance.

Analysis

This approach was much more prone to loose rock this year with a fresh rockfall covering some of the approach. Following behind any party when there is likelihood that loose rocks may be dislodged is always risky. (Source: Brad White, Banff National Park Mountain Safety Specialist)

RAPPEL ERROR – FAULTY USE OF EQUIPMENT, STRANDED, INEXPE-RIENCE, POOR ROUTE RESEARCH
Alberta, Jasper National Park, Morrow Peak

On July 18, MJ and AB left the climbers parking lot at 0930 to climb Morrow Peak via the guide's route. Weather was good but deteriorating slowly by the afternoon with clouds, light winds, and sprinkles. They ascended to the top just below the upper treed bench. They were unaware of the hiking trail down in the treed bench and proceeded to rappel down the route using tree anchors. Their rappel set-up consisted of MJ using an ATC attached to himself with AB connected to him and his rappel device via a daisy chain and screw-lock carabiners. MJ controlled their descent. The carabiner connecting AB to the daisy chain was not locked. Fifteen feet into their second rappel down sloping and benched limestone, the carabiner opened and disconnected from the daisy chain. MJ caught AB with his arm before she could fall. They stopped, sat down, and called 911 using a cellphone. Jasper National Park Public Safety Specialists responded and heli-slung them out to the highway below.

Analysis

They had only been climbing four months. They had no helmets and minimal gear. Continuing on the rappel line down would have led them into much more serious terrain. They did not research the route adequately as they were unaware of the hiking trail down. Despite the situation they created for themselves, stopping and calling for assistance facilitated a positive outcome. (Source: G. Lemke, Public Safety Specialist, Jasper National Park)

FALL ON ROCK, INADEQUATE BELAY
Alberta, Kananaskis Country, Grassi Lakes

On July 25, two climbers were ascending a bolted route on the White Imperialist wall at Grassi Lakes. The lead climber fell from above the fourth bolt. The belay was using an ATC belay device but was unable to hold the leader fall as the rope burned her hand. The leader fell 20 feet landing on his tailbone. Kananaskis Country Public Safety Specialists evacuated the injured climber. (Source: Kananaskis Country Public Safety Program)
(Canadian Editor's Note: There was no indication that equipment failure or faulty use of equipment was a contributing factor.)

FALL ON ROCK, HEAVY PACKS, UNROPED
Alberta, Canadian Rockies, Mount Neptuak

On August 28, a party of seven set out on a club outing to traverse some of the ten peaks from west to east in the Valley of the Ten Peaks, Banff National Park. They had very large packs with bivouac and climbing gear. When nearing the summit of the first peak, Mount Neptuak, one of the party fell over backwards while trying to negotiate the 4th class terrain and tumbled through the large talus below, which, resulted in her breaking her arm. The trip leader called on his cellphone requesting a rescue.

An Alpine Helicopter responded and the patient was slung off. Due to the lateness of the day and the distance from a suitable bivouac spot, the rest of the group was also evacuated back to Wenkchemna Pass and they abandoned their traverse ambitions. (Source: Brad White, Banff National Park Mountain Safety Specialist)

(Canadian Editor's Note: Carrying a heavy pack can make seemingly easy terrain very difficult. This party may have benefited from short-rope or belay. In addition, there can be challenges to managing a larger group on technical terrain.)

SOLO SCRAMBLING, STRANDED
Alberta, Canadian Rockies, Mount Rundle

On September 6, WM was hiking near Banff and headed up the side of Mount Rundle. He climbed up an old streambed and eventually got to the point where he then climbed up difficult terrain that he could not climb down and he could go no further upwards. WM used his cellphone to call for help. Parks Mountain Safety Specialists and an Alpine Helicopters rescue pilot responded. The team was inserted to flatter ground above the cliff and a rescuer was lowered down to WM. The two then climbed up on top rope and all were heli-slung from the mountain.

Analysis

Although cellphones seem to make it almost too easy to call for help at times, there have been numerous fatalities from similar events like this on this same mountain, and had this individual not been able to call, he may have slipped trying to climb up or down with almost certainly fatal consequences. This is another mountain where the detailed scramble route brochure has helped limit the number of incidents like this one. (Source: Brad White, Banff National Park Mountain Safety Specialist)

(Canadian Editor's Note: This is another example of a scrambler moving into technical terrain and requiring evacuation and rescue. It is important to remember that climbing up is often easier than climbing down. Banff National Park reported another similar incident with a solo scrambler caught in technical terrain on Cascade Mountain and requiring a heli-rescue.)

STRANDED – UNDERESTIMATED ROUTE DIFFICULTY, POOR ROUTE RESEARCH
Alberta, Canadian Rockies, Mount Rundle

On September 15, three climbers set out to traverse Mount Rundle in Banff National Park from south to north. They had relatively heavy overnight packs and were prepared for a multi-day outing. After spending two days traversing, they got to a very technical section on the ridge and they climbed up but could not find a way down. At this point they realized that they had underestimated the difficulty of the route and felt that they could not continue or retreat so they phoned for help. Parks Mountain Safety specialists and an Alpine Helicopters rescue pilot responded and the trio were heli-slung off the mountain.

Analysis

Groups should be prepared for self-rescue, which should also include the ability to retreat from a route. Cellphones have made the decision to call for help once over-committed that much easier. (Source: Brad White, Banff National Park Mountain Safety Specialist)

FALL ON ROCK, UNROPED
Alberta, Canadian Rockies, Mount Temple

On September 26, while down-climbing the steep grey rock band on the "tourist route" on Mount Temple, Banff National Park, LR slipped and fell to the scree below seriously breaking his leg. His partner ran down the trail to Moraine Lake to request a rescue. Parks Mountain Safety Specialists and a rescue pilot responded to the scene. Conditions were very windy, but eventually through excellent flying a single rescuer was inserted to the patient and he was packaged and slung off the mountain.

Analysis

Heli-Flight Rescue (HFRS) is the most common method of evacuation employed for most incidents in steep terrain in the Mountain National Parks. It requires only a few highly trained personnel and is quick and efficient. However, it is contingent on good flying weather and it is often only through the great skill of the rescue pilots that the method is possible. A ground evacuation from a spot like this would have been a long and dangerous exercise that would have taken all night and required a crew of at least eight rescuers. Parties should be prepared with adequate first aid training and the ability to stabilize a patient. (Source: Brad White, Banff National Park Mountain Safety Specialist)

STRANDED, LATE START – BENIGHTED, INADEQUATE CLOTHING AND EQUIPMENT, WEATHER
Alberta, Canadian Rockies, Mount Norquay

On October 24, two scramblers started up a difficult scramble on Mount Norquay in Banff National Park at 1300. They reached the ridge top from the ski hill late in the day. The weather had changed from overcast to overcast and snowing lightly. By the time they had descended to the lower crux of the route, they were benighted and conditions had become very slippery with the new snow. They decided to stay put, as they thought they might slip and fall. Their cellphone was low on batteries so they were only able to text message. Their text to a friend at around midnight was, "Ten minutes from car on Norquay and needed help." Then another text that said, "Too icy, sleeping on mtn". The friend called the RCMP who eventually got in contact with Parks dispatch. A Parks Mountain Rescue Specialist was able to climb up in the dark and short rope the two down via easier terrain.

Analysis

The two started late, were not prepared for the length of the route nor were they equipped for the change in weather. They carried no rope or equipment that would have made the descent safe and possible. (Source: Brad White, Banff National Park Mountain Safety Specialist)

(Canadian Editor's Note: Another example of scramblers moving into technical terrain and requiring assistance. Banff National Park also reported one accident where a climber was bouldering on a small fridge sized rock that rolled over and crushed the climber's ankle, which required a heli-evacuation.)

WEATHER, FALL INTO CREVASSE – SNOW BRIDGE FAILED
British Columbia, Purcell Mountains, International Mountain

I was guiding two clients on a ski mountaineering traverse from the Bugaboos to Rogers Pass with the help of an assistant guide. On April 16, we got into camp in Malachite Creek in the early evening. The next day we planned to ski from Malachite Creek to International Basin via Malachite Col, the Carbonate Icefield and International Mountain. It is 12 km in distance and about 800 m elevation gain; we planned to take about 6.5 hours.

That evening we got a forecast via satellite phone that indicated a fast-moving cold front would move through the next afternoon, accompanied with strong winds and intense snowfall (10+ cm) with a rapid improvement the day after. It sounded as if the timing would allow us to get through the serious terrain of the col and the crevasses near International Mountain before the worst of it.

The morning weather observation showed broken skies, -5 C, moderate west winds at ridgetop but no blowing snow, and a steady barometer. We rated snow stability as "Good" and avalanche danger "Low".

We had obvious issues with the forecasted weather, so we planned to move fast. We were out of camp by 8:30 a.m., but by 9:30 a.m. we had flurries and gusty strong winds, with visibility about two km through mist; the front had reached us earlier than expected. We reached Malachite Col at about noon and it was decision time—should we stay or should we go? From here we had about a 2.5 km flat traverse to the crux getting past International Mountain. Visibility was OK although the light was flat; there was about two cm of snow since the morning. If all went well it would take about two hours to easy ground and a sheltered camp. Decision? Go!

In about 1.5 hours, we were approaching the rocks that we needed to get around on International Mountain. We were about 60 m from these rocks.

We would need to either traverse below them on steep slopes or get on top of them and walk a bit to a steep snow ridge that we could descend. The flat icefield suddenly starts tipping into 30+ degrees and there are steep slopes below that end in big ice and rock cliffs. Open crevasses were visible below and ahead there was a shoulder in the ice that would be favourable to forming crevasses.

The weather and snow conditions were changing rapidly. Moderate winds were causing the new snow to start to slab but overall coverage on the glacier was thin; there were areas where the ice was exposed. I had to decide whether thin crevasse bridges or slab avalanches were the greater hazard. If we triggered an avalanche, even a small one, while roped up, it would be disastrous and we would almost certainly all be dragged over the cliffs below. If I took the rope off and fell into a crevasse, it would also be very serious.

The new snow loading combined with the exposed terrain below made me seriously consider taking the rope off. However, there were crevasses nearby, and although there was no indication, we were right in them the terrain was conducive to them. The light was flat, the snowpack was thin, and I had previous beta that there were crevasses here. Although the snow was a bit slabby it was bonding well and in the end I decided to keep the rope on.

Ten steps later, unaware that I was on a bridge due to the poor light, I fell into a crevasse. The crevasse bridge was four m wide, 12 m long and one m thick and I was in the middle of it when it failed all at once. A moment later I was tight on the end of the rope, lying on my side on a steep snow slope in the crevasse with the black maw gaping below me. I had free-fallen about six meters. ER (my assistant guide) was second and had been pulled over, but EH and FB didn't even feel a tug. ER held the fall easily. We couldn't hear each other at all, so she decided not to do a tractor pull and quickly made an anchor.

This was a good thing, I was uncomfortably pinned against the snow by the rope and it would have been a mess if they had started hauling on me right away. It was a struggle, but I managed to clip everything to the rope: ski poles first, then pack and finally skis. Once that was all off, I could stand up and put my pack back on before climbing up the very steep snow slope to the lip, hauling my poles and skis. Once ER saw me there, she self-belayed to the edge with a prusik and I handed all my gear to her before getting a hand out. The whole thing took maybe ten minutes.

Then the fun started. We were suddenly in a full-blown blizzard and it took quite some time to work our way above and onto the rocks and navigate down the steep snow ridge to get to the easier ground beyond.

Analysis

So what did I learn?

—I like to have an experienced helper along whenever possible on trips involving avalanche terrain and crevasses, and it paid off this time round as it was a relief to know there was someone on the surface who could get me out if need be.

—I was using a 45-m-long low-stretch 9-mm rope (rather than a dynamic climbing rope) and there were no issues with impact force, both ER and I didn't feel much of a jerk when I hit the end of the rope, and I was free falling for several meters. We also had another 35 m rope that EH was carrying, so we had plenty of cord to play with.

—I don't recommend a tractor pull unless you can communicate: if the victim is in an awkward position you could easily hurt them by blindly tugging on the rope.

—I worried a bit initially that I had almost taken the rope off due to the possibility of a slab avalanche in that exposed terrain but in the end I realize I came up with the right decision and that's a positive thing.

We had made a series of decisions before getting to that crevasse and I think they were all reasonable ones. In the end, we had to rely on our last line of defence on the glacier—the rope, but everything worked the way it was supposed to. We are never going to be entirely risk-free out there and this incident showed me that if I use all the tools I have available, I could have a scrape and walk away from it, although I don't plan on making a habit of it! (Source: Mark Klassen, ACMG / IFMGA Mountain Guide)

(Canadian Editor's Note: While this isn't an accident in the sense that it resulted in injury, it is an excellent first-hand account of a situation that provides insight into some decision making and risk management while travelling in the mountains.)

FALL ON SNOW – UNABLE TO SELF-ARREST, INADEQUATE EQUIPMENT, INEXPERIENCE,

British Columbia, Canadian Rockies, Castle Glacier

On Aug 3rd J.C. (22) and A.T. (24), on a day off from their university geology field trip, left their camp located at the base of Castle Glacier to ascend a nearby peak. They had to cross a crevassed glacier and ascend a loose rock rib to the summit. They brought crampons, bear spray, and a daypack. From the summit they decided to descend via a different route.

Descending the peak at 1230, they encountered very broken and friable rock that led them to a snow gully. At the top of the snow slope the party decided to put their crampons on. A.T. had one crampon on when his pack started to slide away. He lunged for the pack, lost his balance and began to slide uncontrollably down the snow slope. He hit a rock and continued sliding and eventually fell into a ten meters deep bergschrund. J.C. down climbed and entered the bergschrund from the side to assist A.T. Together, they walked out of the side of the bergschrund. A.T. did lose consciousness momentarily during his slide after hitting the rock, broke his wrist, and received several minor scalp lacerations.

The party was able to call out on their satellite phone to the helicopter company that flew the camp in. The helicopter company initially responded but quickly realized that a heli-sling rescue would be required. The Provincial Emergency Program was contacted who then requested the assistance of Jasper National Park (JNP) Public Safety Specialists. JNP Public Safety Specialists responded and, using map coordinates from the helicopter company, located the subjects and safely evacuated them using a heli-sling.

Analysis

The climbers had limited to no experience in glaciated alpine terrain. They had no rope, ice axes, helmets, harness, only crampons and daypack. However, having a satellite phone was invaluable to call for assistance. As a result, they were successfully rescued from their predicament. (Source: G. Lemke, Public Safety Specialist, Jasper National Park)

FALLING ROCK — PULLED OFF BY LEAD CLIMBER
British Columbia, Bugaboos Provincial Park, Snowpatch Spire

On August 15, a climber was climbing the last pitch of Sunshine Crack (IV 5.10+) on Snowpatch Spire. The lead climber pulled off a rock about twice the size of his torso, which hit the belayer on his lower back. The climbers self-evacuated themselves to the Conrad Kain hut, even though the injured climber was having difficulty maintaining consciousness on the rappels. Columbia Valley Search and Rescue evacuated the climber. (Source: Tay Hanson, Senior Park Ranger)

FALL ON ROCK, PLACED NO PROTECTION
British Columbia, Bugaboos Provincial Park, Eastpost Spire

On August 31st, a climber was leading up a line on the NW side of Eastpost when he slipped and fell approximately 40 feet to the ledge below. He had not placed any protection.

Injuries were assessed as being a broken ankle, some lacerations and potential concussion. Climbers at Applebee responded and provided first aid, then radioed for help. Columbia Valley Search and Rescue evacuated the climber. (Source: Tay Hanson, Senior Park Ranger)

FALL ON ICE, SOLO CLIMBING
British Columbia, Canadian Rockies, Haffner Creek

On December 18, CC was solo ice climbing in Haffner Creek in Kootenay National Park when he fell and sustained injuries to his shoulder and collarbone. A nearby UIAGM Mountain guide came to his assistance and called for help on his radio. The patient was able to walk with help and the guide brought him to the trailhead where the ambulance picked him up. (Source: Brad White, Banff National Park Mountain Safety Specialist)

UNITED STATES

CLIMBING ALONE, UNROPED, INADEQUATE FOOD AND EQUIPMENT, INEXPERIENCE
Alaska, Mount McKinley, West Buttress

On May 21, Gerald Myers (41), a member of a private expedition of four, was reported as overdue on a solo summit attempt of Mount McKinley from the 14,200-foot camp. Without prior consultation with his partners and unbeknown to them, he departed the camp around 4:30 a.m. on May 19 with no stove, shovel, or bivouac gear and with an unknown amount of food. He retrieved his skis, which had been previously cached, from the 17,200-foot high camp, and was last positively seen around 4:00 p.m. near the 18,700-foot elevation by two separate climbing groups descending from aborted summit attempts because of high winds. One of those groups and another separate group successfully attained the summit the following day, and upon arrival back at the 17,200-foot camp, one of the expeditions' members mistakenly reported that he had seen the missing climber on the summit ridge. This mistake wasn't identified until the expedition had descended to the 7,200-foot camp on the evening of May 24, where he was interviewed.

Search operations were initiated on the morning of May 21 when it was determined that the climber had failed to descend to the high camp. During this endeavor, both fixed and rotary wing aircraft were used to search and photograph the high reaches of the mountain, including the alternate routes that a climber might use to ski or hike down. The aerial search totaled 30.19 hours, of which 18.09 hours were from fixed wing aircraft and 12.1 were from helicopters. During these flights, 6,025 high-resolution photographs were taken and analyzed for clues.

On May 26, in light of the Myer's minimal supplies and the sub-zero temperatures and high winds prevalent on the mountain during the search period, search managers concluded that survival was outside the window of possibility. Active search operations were terminated with no pertinent clues being found as the whereabouts of Myers.

Analysis

Many decisions were made by Myers and his expedition as a whole that likely contributed to his disappearance. The first was the rapid ascent that the expedition made to the 17,200-foot camp. This may have predisposed Myers to contracting HACE/HAPE while high on the mountain. The second was the Myer's decision to attempt a solo ascent to the summit from the 14,200-foot camp. Not only was it a spur-of-the-moment decision, it also left him traveling alone without any support in the event of an accident. Myers apparently did not comprehend the difficulty in conducting a sum-

15

mit attempt from the 14,200-foot camp. Traveling solo and his failure to carry any survival gear or equipment that would enable him to construct a shelter surely was a major contributing factor to his death. Myers also lacked experience with extreme high altitude and would not have known his physical limits at that elevation. If he had, he might have recognized the futility of his attempt and turned around.

It will never be known why he did not turn around after talking with the descending climbers on May 19. It can only be hypothesized that he did not recognize the severity of the situation and was driven to reach or photograph the summit at all costs. An increasing number of climbers are traveling solo and/or unroped on Denali, which is a disturbing trend. (Source for all Denali National Park incidents here and below: Denali National Park Rangers.)

HAPE, FAILURE TO TURN BACK
Alaska, Mount McKinley, West Buttress

On May 11, a guided client (52) first started experiencing a productive cough and wet lung sounds at 11,200 feet. After a carry from 11,200 feet to 13,500 feet, he felt a bit better and wanted to move up to the 14,200-foot camp with the rest of the team. He moved very slowly up to 14,200 feet on May 13 and on May 14 barely participated in any camp activities due to fatigue and feeling ill.

On May 15, a guide brought him to the Ranger camp, as he was exhibiting signs and symptoms of High Altitude Pulmonary Edema. After 24 hours of monitoring his conditions, rangers and NPS Physician-advisor determined that the client was unfit to descend to base camp. He was evacuated via the NPS Contract helicopter without incident.

Analysis

HAPE is a common ailment for McKinley climbers. It can be life-threatening, but it can also be avoided. This group ascended from 11,200-foot to 14,200-foot on their seventh day on the glacier, a very reasonable and moderate pace. However, this schedule was still too fast for the client to properly acclimatize. More time spent at lower camps could certainly have helped. Additionally, sick climbers rarely get better on McKinley due to the combination of environmental factors, altitude, and effort required to climb. A helicopter evacuation could have been avoided if the client had decided to descend from 11,200-foot camp rather than to choose to move up.

FALL ON SNOW, CLIMBING UNROPED, POOR POSITION
Alaska, Mount McKinley, West Buttress

On May 26, a climber (33) was descending un-roped with his team members along the ridge below Washburn's Thumb at approximately 16,500 feet. At this location the terrain forces the route off the ridge onto the North side of the buttress.

The climber encountered an ascending guided expedition on this steeper, off fall-line, traversing slope. Though the guided group was placing snow pickets as fall protection on this terrain feature, he decided not to wait until the trail was clear but rather to descend the traverse above the guided group. While descending the traverse, he lost his footing, fell, and became entangled in the guided group's rope. He suffered a dislocated shoulder.

NPS Rangers lowered him from the base of the fixed-lines to the 14,200-foot camp and attempted, but could not reduce, his shoulder dislocation.

After a span of seven days of non-flyable weather, he was evacuated on the eighth day by NPS helicopter without incident.

Analysis

The terrain where the climber fell is an off-fall line, left upward-trending traverse on about a 40-degree slope. Although the climbing is not difficult, it can be awkward when carrying large loads. Often the trail is hard-packed, uneven ice, with the fall line being down towards the Peters Glacier. Guided groups use a rope and place up to three snow pickets for protection in this section. With up to a 1,500-foot potential fall down to the Peters Glacier, climbing here unprotected has potential for injury or death. A lot like a micro-Autobahn (a terrain feature located above 17,200-foot camp leading up to Denali Pass), this spot is generally underestimated and its consequences often over looked.

The climber's decision not to use a rope for this section resulted in a serious injury. The ridge was crowded with slower moving guided groups on their way up. He fell into another group that was using the appropriate technique of being roped and placing protection. He could have caused a major catastrophe if he had dislodged this group. Climbing the crowded West Buttress demands patience and respect for other climbers. Haste put both himself and others in a dangerous position.

It is worth noting that this was one of three similar incidents at this same location.

"INTERFERING WITH AGENCY FUNCTION" – UNNECESSARY HELICOPTER EVACUATION
Alaska, Mount McKinley, West Buttress

On June 1st, a female Lithuanian climber (47) was air evacuated from the 14,200-foot camp on Denali's West Buttress. NPS rangers made numerous attempts to help her descend under her own power, but she refused all options except for air evacuation. Because of her actions, she placed NPS Rangers and others in a potentially hazardous situation. The climber was cited under 36 CFR 2.32 (a)(3)—"Interfering with Agency Function," which carries a maximum sentence of $5,000 and six months of jail time.

She left the country before the date of her court appearance.

Analysis

The climber's chief complaint was a minor foot injury caused by over use and poorly fitting boots. She underestimated the challenges of climbing the West Buttress on Denali and the necessity of self-reliance in the remote mountains of Alaska. She did not understand the risk involved with rescue operations, including air evacuation from 14,200 feet. She also did not understand the safety hazard she imposed on rescue personnel and other climbers. The hazardous situation that she created was difficult to manage and had serious potential to place a lot of people at risk. Failure to see rescue operations in Alaska as different from areas where the risks of rescue may be more easily mitigated is negligent. She was air evacuated because of the potential risk she created for those around her at the 14,200-foot camp.

The following excerpt was taken directly out of the Mountaineering in Denali National Park and Preserve Registration Requirements, Safety Rules and Regulations booklet. This booklet is required reading as part of the registration process. During the orientation given on May 21 in Talkeetna, all members of her expedition were asked if they had read the booklet and all indicated they had. The following is in the section labeled "Search and Rescue Requirements":

"It is the policy of Denali National Park and Preserve to assist those in need, when, in the opinion of park personnel apprised of the situation, it is necessary, appropriate, within the reasonable skill and technical capability of park personnel, and provides searchers and rescuers with a reasonable margin of safety. Search and Rescue Operations are conducted on a discretionary basis. The level and necessity of the response is determined by field personnel based on their evaluation of the situation. Rescuer safety is always our first priority. Denali National Park and Preserve expects park visitors to exhibit a degree of self-reliance and responsibility for their own safety commensurate with the degree of the activities they undertake. A climbing party high on Denali or other Arctic mountains cannot depend on any assistance in the event of an emergency. Due to complexity of a rescue it could be days before rescue personnel could arrive on scene for a rescue. For all practical purposes, a climbing party is alone and must depend upon its own resources if an emergency situation arises."

The most disconcerting aspects of this incident were the wave of people affected and the level of risk caused by a very minor situation. It is frustrating to the many who were involved that she decided to give up. Her injury was such that she could have walked down under her own power, but she refused to do so. The effort and energy expended on this climber put the NPS Rangers in a difficult and potentially dangerous position had there been another true emergency. It became obvious that the only person she was concerned about was herself.

The expenses for the NPS rescue helicopter are continually criticized. To take advantage of this life-saving tool only jeopardizes its use in the future for true emergencies. On a mountain that demands respect and teamwork, she caused her teammate and the NPS unnecessary hardship and made it obvious that she did not understand what the expected ethics are in mountaineering endeavors.

FALL ON ROCK, WEATHER, INEXPERIENCE
Alaska, Moose's Tooth, Ham and Eggs

On May 11, a climber fell about 60 feet while climbing the "Ham and Eggs" route on the Moose's Tooth. He sustained tibia/fibula fractures, with ankle and metatarsal dislocations of his left leg and foot. Other climbers on the route and in the area organized his rescue and evacuation. Once lowered, he was flown out the same day to Talkeetna where he was evaluated by an NPS Ranger before going to the hospital.

The following edited report was filed at the Talkeetna Ranger Station by one of the climbers that took charge of the accident on May 20.

"On May 11, we set off to climb Ham and Eggs at 4:00 a.m. One party was ahead of us. As we progressed up the couloir, on the third pitch the wind picked up and spindrift started pouring down the route like a fire hose. My partner led the third pitch. We were surprised by the rotten quality of the ice, but she was able to place multiple pieces of protection, including rock pro. I led up the fourth pitch, pulling the bulge with the heavy spindrift coming down, thinking, 'If this gets worse, we will retreat.' Just then my partner mentioned the party below us had an accident. I brought her up and we decided to retreat due to the conditions and also because I am a nurse and we knew there was a bad accident below. Upon rapping, I came upon the injured climber prusiking up the route with one leg. His climbing partner was in shock and not doing much, so I decided to take control of the situation. I set up a rap-assisted web system [buddy rappel] while I rapped with a prusik backup and an overhead belay backup. With help from the party above us that also had retreated due to the weather conditions, we all worked down four rappels to the ground. Other climbers on the ground brought a sled over to lower him down to the snowfield."

Analysis

The climber commented that the weather and inexperience contributed to this incident. She also indicated that she thought the ice was not worth placing a screw, whereas her partner did get multiple pieces of rock and ice pro in.

FALL ON SNOW/ICE
Alaska, Mount McKinley, West Rib

On June 11, two climbers (36 and 39, US) died of injuries sustained during a fall while ascending the West Rib route. Though the origin of the fall was not witnessed, it is believed to have begun at approximately 19,200 feet. The two climbers, who were roped together, were witnessed falling at approximately the 16,000-foot level to the end of their fall around the 14,500-foot level. Subsequent to the report of the fall, a National Park Service hasty team and a group of private climbers immediately responded to the accident site and found that they had died due to injuries sustained during the fall. The bodies where recovered from the scene and evacuated to Talkeetna for transfer to the State of Alaska Medical Examiner.

Analysis

Though it is not now and never will be known what exactly caused this tragic fall, what is known about the two individuals and circumstances involved make the reality of this accident challenging to understand. The facts that are known are that both climbers were experienced and had a history of making the right decisions when venturing into the mountains. On this climb they routinely placed protection on moderate and steep terrain.

It was a beautiful day and conditions were reported to be ideal for climbing. Their ascent rate was within acceptable norms, and neither climber is known to have been compromised by altitude illness. They had food, water, and all the necessary equipment. The area from which they fell is no more difficult than they had previously climbed and the steepness of the terrain was well within their level of skill and experience

One question that has been asked is why did they not have protection in place. Unfortunately that cannot be answered by anyone except the two climbers. Could it have made a difference? Maybe. It is accurate to say that the decision of when and where to place protection is of a subjective nature and that depending on the given circumstances, a climber may make one decision today and a entirely different one tomorrow, neither being right or wrong. In this case, the decisions of when and where to place protection were made by two cautious and competent climbers who did not define success by summiting, two who took the challenges of mountaineering seriously and did not underestimate the associated risk or the magnitude of climbing Denali.

INADEQUATE FOOD, NO WORKING STOVES
Alaska, Mount McKinley, Cassin Ridge

On June 11, two climbers (38 and 40) attempting the Cassin Ridge requested a rescue when they ran out of food and water and had no working stoves. They called on FRS and reported that they had "no energy and we cannot go up." At this time they asked, "We wonder if possible a rescue."

A helicopter launched around 1830 from Talkeetna. The climbers were located on a steep slope, and so the drop target was a lower-angled garden of rocks about 100 feet above them. The first drop hit the target perfectly, but it proved to be too steep and the supplies slid down the entirety of Denali's Southwest Face. The second drop, positioned just above the first, did exactly the same. Papa Hotel (name of the helicopter) descended to base camp to re-supply and reassess its target. Two more loads were created, both of which were tied on to the end of 100-foot ropes. Papa Hotel ascended and lowered the first load directly to the climbers, who retrieved it without problem. Papa Hotel then descended to base camp and then returned to Talkeetna.

The climbers used the re-supply to ascend the rest of the Cassin the next day. They then safely descended the West Buttress route and arrived 24 hours after reaching the top of the Cassin. Upon returning to base camp, the two were observed to be in good spirits—with much energy and no apparent injuries or illnesses.

Analysis
In this situation there appeared to be cultural/national differences over what "emergencies" constitute proper grounds for a rescue. There also appeared to be different expectations for the attainability and possibility of rescue on Denali. Denali Mountaineering Rangers attempt to educate climbers that rescues are dangerous, difficult, and not very commonly possible. However, many climbers still assume that if things go bad, they'll be picked up by the helicopter without any problem.

We hope that further education and using this situation as a lesson will prevent this from happening again to them and others.

AVALANCHE, FALL ON SNOW — SKI MOUNTAINEERING, IGNORED RECENT AVALANCHE ACTIVITY, MISJUDGED SNOWPACK, USING SKI-CUTS TO ESTIMATE STABILITY, TRYING TO STICK TO A SCHEDULE
Alaska, Mount McKinley, West Buttress, Rescue Gully
On June 25, a climber (34) set out from 14,200-foot camp with her three teammates, intending to ski a line above 17,200-foot camp known as "Thunderbird". As the team was climbing on the ridge between the fixed lines at 16,200-feet and the 17,200-foot camp, they became concerned with weather conditions up higher on the mountain. They arrived at 17,200-foot camp in high winds. They talked about the conditions and decided not ski "Thunderbird" but to ski down from 17,200-foot camp via the Rescue Gulley instead. The team worked their way down through the steep entrance of the Rescue Gulley and regrouped at the mouth of it to dig a snow pit and evaluate both snow conditions and the terrain below.

Based on their analysis of the snow conditions, the team decided to continue into the open terrain below the Rescue Gulley with plans of skiing one at a time. Being one of the stronger skiers, the climber in question was the first to go. She skied approximately 500 meters straight down, where she triggered an avalanche that swept her off her skis. At first, she slid approximately 200 meters trying to self-arrest and stay above the debris, but after sliding, she began to tumble another 100 meters before coming to a stop on top of the debris. Her initial assessment of herself was that she had a small laceration on the top of her head and an injury to her left knee. She was unable to ski out, so she called the National Park Service for assistance.

About 1830, at the 14,200-foot camp, an NPS Ranger and four patrol volunteers observed the climber begin her ski descent and trigger the avalanche she was caught in. The ranger set up a spotting scope to observe her after she stopped tumbling to see if she was in need of assistance. Before she had called, the ranger observed her stand up after the event and try to sideslip on her skis down the debris field. It was apparent that she had some type of lower leg injury, which led the ranger to have his patrol volunteers gear up as a hasty team and stand by. At 1845, there was an FRS radio call from a climber at the base of the fixed lines who had voice contact with the injured climber. The contact person stated that she was asking for assistance and informed the ranger of the climber's injuries.

The ranger organized four climbers from the 14,200-foot camp to assist his patrol volunteers in a lowering from the patient's location to the 14,200-foot camp. She was directed to stay where she was while a rescue team was organized. The rescue team traveled up the debris field created by the avalanche in order to stay off of other potentially loaded slopes surrounding the patient. When the rescue team arrived on scene, a medic performed an initial assessment, which confirmed a laceration on top of the head that had stopped bleeding, and an injury to the patient's left knee. She was packaged in a sleeping bag for warmth and lowering began with the Cascade Litter at 2120. The lowering team conducted three 200-meter single rope pitches on moderate/low angle terrain to get the patient down to the medical tent at 14,200-feet. Here she was reassessed. It was determined that the injury to her knee was not conducive to skiing down the mountain under her own power. At 0900 on June 26, the park helicopter was called to fly her to base camp the next morning, where she waited to meet up with the rest of her team who were skiing down from the 14,200-foot camp.

Analysis

Skiing off of the West Buttress route and in and round the 14,000-foot camp has gained popularity over the last few years. In 2007 a group of friends based out of the 14,200-foot camp for a 14-day trip were able to ski many classic lines as well as a few first descents. Their trip was characterized by a series of storms that created stable conditions favorable for skiing. This year Denali was again the goal of at least eight expeditions focused on skiing big lines. The 2009 skiing conditions were much different and were characterized early on by icy hard-pack snow and unstable wind slabs toward the end.

The most significant components in this incident were ignoring the recent avalanche activity, misjudging the spatial variability of the snowpack, underestimation of scale of the terrain, and team dynamics. All were very experienced skiers with significant collective knowledge of avalanche formation, mitigation, and snowpack stability. Storm totals are difficult to calculate with the limited availability of wind-sheltered areas, but best estimates were approximately 18 inches with moderate wind transport. There had been a climber-triggered avalanche the day before on the fixed-lines adjacent to the descent line. This size two avalanche slid on an early season ice layer with a crown height of the storm total of approximately 18 inches. The skiers were dusted by the powder cloud from this avalanche, so they were well aware of the instabilities in the snowpack.

When the skiers entered into the gully, they used ski cuts as a method for testing the stability of the snow. They found no instabilities and much less snow in the gully. This is common for the top of the Rescue Gully because of the way the wind funnels through the terrain. Ski cuts, although effective in soft slabs and loose snow, lose their effectiveness as soon as they are not penetrating to the bed surface. Ski-cutting large slopes with high consequences is a dangerous practice that will in time catch even experts off guard.

Their snow pit showed no significant instabilities and was dug at the bottom of the Gully as the slope fans out. The terrain changes from a small more easily managed gully to a large, unsupported, open slope with no safe areas. What they failed to recognize was that their snow pit did not represent the snowpack on a subtle, wind loaded, convex roll lower on the slope. Their methods for testing for instabilities, ski cuts, and their snow pit were un-representational of the larger more dangerous slope below. Because their tests showed stable snow with no wind slab, they assumed the entire slope to be the same and did not take into account the high degree of spatial variability represented on this slope.

They also underestimated the size and consequences of the terrain. From the 14,200-foot camp and their climb up to the fixed lines, they had identified the subtle convex roll on the slope and agreed to stay away from it. Once the injured climber exited the gully and the slope widened, she indicated that she lost track of her position on the slope and could not tell where the convex roll was. As she committed to the slope, the snow changed from loose, manageable snow to a supportable wind slab.

There were obvious signs of instability. The terrain is characterized as a large, open, unsupported slope with a small convex roll, and because of the elevation and wind, a high degree of spatial variability. All of these are red flags that when the team members were asked later, each recognized them at some point. So why did they over look these obvious clues? All members of the team were highly motivated expert skiers and wanted to ski. The snow conditions up until this storm cycle had not been good and now it was excellent. A few days before, a team of skiers had successfully skied the Rescue Gulley early on in the storm. But for this team, it was the last day of their trip and they had not skied any of their big objectives yet. The schedule, therefore, dictated their attempt.

(Editor's Note: While the objective for this team was to ski on a big mountain, this incident fits the category of ski mountaineering because of the techniques and equipment required to get to and from the objective. We will decide on a case by case basis as to which incidents resulting from skiing the big and steep will qualify for this category.)

VARIOUS MEDICAL PROBLEMS
Alaska, Mount McKinley

During the 2009 season, there were several medical incidents (including the HAPE report above). These included a guided client (41) with significant enough chest pain to be evacuated be helicopter; a guided client (31) with extreme fatigue and very low O2 saturation at the 17,200-foot camp who descended under his own power to basecamp; a guided client (49) who collapsed up arrival at the 9,500-foot camp after experiencing "extreme" pain in his chest (sledded back to basecamp, evacuated, and diagnosed with two "major heart blockages"); and a guided client, William Hearne (61) from New York, who collapsed and died at 13,500 feet.

Analysis

The expedition on which Mr. Hearne died took three days to move from Base Camp at 7,200 feet to the 11,200-foot camp. They did this making single carries. The expedition took one rest day at the 11,200-foot camp and then the following day made a carry of gear to 13,500 feet. When the team moved from their 9,500-foot camp to the 11,200-foot camp, Mr. Hearne needed the assistance of his guide to carry his gear sled. He had also exhibited fatigue on the day of his collapse and needed assistance with his backpack on the last hill that leads up toward Windy Corner.

Fatigue is common during these early carries. The distances are not great, but the amount food and gear that are required for 21 days on the mountain make the loads heavy. Elevation also begins to be a significant factor contributing to many individuals experiencing fatigue above the 11,200-foot camp.

From the people interviewed after the incident, it appears that Mr. Hearne was not subjected to any abnormal ascent regime or excessive physical stress. Friends and family also indicated that he was in excellent physical condition.

From 1995-2008, there have been 282 climbers 60 or over who have completed climbs on Denali safely. There have been 1,508 over the age of 50. Of the five heart-related deaths since 1932 to present, only one has been over the age of 59. With only one exception, an interesting note is that all of these have been since 2006.

(Editor's Note: It is not unusual to have a variety of medical incidents in this extreme environment. The analysis provided for the last incident mentioned covers many of the important factors.

Another piece information for 2009 is that 1,052 climbers registered to attempt the mountain.)

LOOSE ROCKS (SEDIMENTARY) CAME OFF, FALL ON ROCK
Arizona, Mount Lemmon, Chimney Rock

On April 15 I (Tom Thrall, 58) was on the fourth day of a week-long climbing trip with my friend WG (69) on Mount Lemmon near Tucson. It was very windy that day, so we decided to stay low on the mountain. Two other climbers we had met at the campground that morning offered to join us and we headed down the highway to Chimney Rock. WG did a fine job negotiating the unusual climbing on the first pitch of the Standard Route (5.6), which I seconded and then traversed far left over to the anchors on the arête below the second pitch. Meanwhile, GP and SR climbed the first pitch behind us on a separate rope.

When I arrived at the arête, the wind velocity was extreme, and I found it difficult to even stand without holding on to the anchors. The guidebook had mentioned a "5.8 variation" to the second pitch, which looked a bit more wind protected, so I decided to give it a try instead. After scrambling up into an alcove, I found myself at the bottom of a somewhat rotten appearing face that rose steeply for about twenty five feet before the angle backed off a bit. There was a discontinuous crack in the face with what looked like several reasonable placements for protection. The first moves went well, and I got in a TCU about seven feet up and then a bomber Camalot about five feet above that. Moving past the Camalot, I found that the rock deteriorated significantly. I was about three feet below my next pro placement on small ledges that were literally crumbling beneath my fingers and toes. I considered down-climbing, but that felt very insecure. There was a larger hold tempting me a couple of moves away that would allow me to rest and place protection, so I decided to go for it.

As I pulled up into my next stance, my left handhold came loose and I was suddenly airborne. I hit the ledge at the base of the face with considerable force, landing on my right side. I was wearing a helmet, did not lose consciousness, and was able to take stock of my situation. I noticed the rope was tight up to the Camalot, which had held its placement well and had presumably absorbed some of the force of the fall. I called down to my friends, and soon one of the climbers we met came up to check me over, set up an anchor and a chest harness, and lower me down the cliff. The rescue went smoothly and we were on our way to the hospital in what seemed like a very short time. WG and our two new friends all remained calm and efficient throughout the rescue, and I am deeply indebted for their kind and competent assistance.

At the hospital I was found to have a stable pelvic fracture with a large hematoma around my right hip, a maxillary fracture with loss of several teeth, facial lacerations, and a severe fracture/dislocation of my right wrist, which required open reduction and screw fixation. There remains a possibility that I will have some permanent nerve damage in my right hand from the injury.

Analysis

In retrospect I would have been better off attempting to down-climb when I first recognized that the rock was becoming dangerously rotten. I may have fallen anyway, but would likely not have hit the ledge and been injured as badly. (Source: Tom Thrall)

FALSE ALARM
Arizona, Grand Canyon

On the evening of September 23rd, rangers began a search for hikers who repeatedly activated their rented SPOT satellite-tracking device. The GEOS Emergency Response Center in Houston reported that someone in the group of four hikers—two men and their two teenaged sons—had pressed the "help" button on their SPOT unit. The coordinates for the signal placed the group in a remote section of the park, most likely on the challenging Royal Arch loop. Due to darkness and the remoteness of the location, rangers were unable to reach them via helicopter until the following morning. When found, they'd moved about a mile and a half to a water source. They declined rescue, as they'd activated the device due to their lack of water. Later that same evening, the same SPOT device was again activated, this time using the "911" button. Coordinates placed them less than a quarter mile from the spot where searchers had found them that morning. Once again, nightfall prevented a response by park helicopter, so an Arizona DPS helicopter whose crew utilized night vision goggles was brought in. They found that the members of the group were concerned about possible dehydration because the water they'd found tasted salty, but no actual emergency existed. The helicopter crew declined their request for a night evacuation but provided them with water before departing. On the following morning, another SPOT "help" activation came in from the group. This time they were flown out by park helicopter. All four refused medical assessment or treatment. The group's leader had reportedly hiked once at the Grand Canyon; the other adult had no Grand Canyon and very little backpacking experience. When asked what they would have done without the SPOT device, the leader stated, "We would have never attempted this hike."

The group leader was issued a citation for creating a hazardous condition—36 CFR 2.34(a)(4). (Source: Brandon Torres, Canyon District Shift Supervisor, from an entry found in the Morning Report, October 21, 2009) *(Editor's Note: While not a climbing accident, this episode is included to illustrate the misuse of ever more sophisticated and available technologies. We are not seeing a lot of this inappropriate use in the climbing world yet, but we are certainly seeing an increase in the use of cellphones for calling in for rescue help.)*

VARIOUS FALLS – UNABLE TO SELF-ARREST WHILE GLISSADING, FAULTY USE OF CRAMPONS (3), OUT OF CONTROL FALL
California, Mount Shasta

On January 18, a climber in Avalanche Gulch attempted to glissade on hard snow with crampons on, beginning at 11,500 feet. He quickly lost control and went into a slide/tumble for 500 vertical feet. He suffered an ankle fracture and other minor injuries. He was assisted by another climbing party and some local skiers/snowboarders to lower elevations. He was transported by toboggan by a USFS Climbing Ranger to the trailhead.

On May 24, a 52-year-old male sprained his ankle while glissading near Lake Helen at the 10,400-foot level. A climbing ranger assessed the injury, taped the ankle, and the subject continued down with help from his party.

On May 30, a climbing ranger stopped two out of control climbers sliding through the Red Banks at 12,400 feet. The ranger assisted them through the remainder of the chimney.

On June 7, a 46-year-old male was glissading down Avalanche Gulch around the 11,500-foot level with crampons on. A crampon caught on the snow and as a result, the man sustained open fractures to his tibia and fibula. Bystanders, including two MDs and several climbing guides, called 911 and stabilized him. Three climbing rangers responded to the scene with rescue gear and packaged him for transport via CHP Helicopter H-16 to Mercy Mt. Shasta for treatment.

On June 28, after observing several climbers sliding out of control through the Red Banks chimney around the 12,400-foot level, rangers instructed several dozen climbers in proper use of the ice ax.

On August 1, a 46-year-old female fell below just below the Red Banks at 12,400 feet. A party member dove on top of her to stop her fall. In the process, he cut her thigh with his crampon, resulting in a two-and-a-half inch laceration. A climbing ranger met her just below Lake Helen, assessed her condition, carried her gear, and escorted her to Bunny Flat.

On October 31, a 43-year-old male climber was reported to have a fractured hip after falling from the 12,500-foot level in Avalanche Gulch. This occurred during a full-moon Halloween climb with his partner. He fell/slid approximately 1,200 vertical feet to 11,300 feet and was then assisted to 10,800 feet.

He had a helmet, crampons and an ice ax, but was unable to self-arrest. He had climbed the route before, but only during summer conditions. The route had two feet of very firm snow with boulders protruding, creating conditions more dangerous than during the peak climbing season in May and June when the snow is ten to fifteen deep and few rocks are exposed.

He was left at 10,800 feet while his partner hiked out to get assistance. A CHP helicopter began looking for the him around 1100 on November 1, but was unable to find him. A USFS climbing ranger ascended, following crampon tracks, and found the climber at 1120 huddled in a clump of rocks. He was stabilized and then hoisted by the CHP helicopter and flown to Bunny Flat trailhead (7,000 feet) and transferred to the PHI medical helicopter, which transported him to the Mercy Medical Center.

Analysis

(Editor's Note: Climbing Ranger Eric White sent forward his summary of search, rescue, and public assistance for 2009. No statistics in terms of our ANAM format were included. I gleaned the above narratives from the 29 sent forward. The basic data have been entered into the tables. Below is an edited excerpt from the Season Summary.)

The seasonal precipitation was 92 percent of normal and snow surveys below tree line were around 85 percent of normal. We had a late start to the winter, followed by a fairly schizophrenic pattern of cold storms with warm periods in between. An unusually wet spring gave the upper mountain snowpack a big boost and so greatly improved the late spring skiing and prolonged the summer climbing season. Due to these conditions, Mount Shasta had a fairly average climbing season and a great deal more climbers than in the past three drier and shorter seasons.

Avalanche Gulch, the standard route, remained in good condition well into July and attracted the bulk of the spring/summer climbing use. As has been the case for the past several seasons, Clear Creek became the route of choice late in the summer and into the early fall.

In addition to the 27 climbing/hiking related incidents, there were also five reported human-caused avalanches. Four of them resulted in the subjects being caught and carried by the debris and one caused the subject to be nearly entirely buried in the debris. Four occurred on May 9 within approximately 30 minutes of each other. (Source: Eric White, Climbing Ranger/Avalanche Specialist)

AVALANCHE
California, Yosemite National Park, Half Dome
On Sunday, March 15, an experienced South Korean mountain climber Jun Ho Wang (38) was on his way down for more supplies to support his team's winter attempt on Half Dome when he was swept more than 100 meters down a rocky approach to the granite face by an avalanche. Two friends who were nearby tended to him and cut Wang a flat ledge the size of a twin bed out of the ice topping the rock where he could rest wrapped in three sleeping bags. He endured about 16 hours in an icy, low-lying gully before he was plucked from the monolith by a helicopter crew Tuesday morning and flown to safety.

Park officials said he was alert and responsive. Wang was flown to Doctor's Medical Center in Modesto to be treated for a fractured left wrist and multiple breaks in his left leg. He was in a stable condition by Tuesday afternoon, according to hospital staff.
Analysis
"Most people in an avalanche don't survive," said Eric Gabriel, an incident commander for the search and rescue team. "This gentleman not only survived a 100-meter slide, but survived through the night in freezing temperatures."

"It could have been a lot worse, but he was well prepared," said Sean Pence, a manager at Yosemite Medical Clinic, where Wang was evaluated before being flown out of the park. "He had great equipment and his equipment probably saved his life." (Source From an AP post and John Dill, NPS Ranger, Yosemite National Park)

FALL ON ROCK (2), NO HARD HAT
California, Joshua Tree National Park, Hidden Valley
About 4:00 p.m. on March 15, Curtis "Woody" Stark (67) and Alfred Kuok (44) were climbing in an area near the Hidden Valley nature trail. The trail is a popular destination for both day hikers and rock climbers. Stark was the lead climber on the Great Burrito formation and was being followed by Kuok. Stark experienced some difficulty with his climb and began to descend. During the descent, he lost his grip and fell. As he fell, Stark struck Kuok, causing him to fall as well. Kuok's protection held, arresting his fall,

but Stark continued to fall, suffering fatal head injuries when he struck the ground. It's estimated that he fell about 100 feet.

Two other rock climbers immediately responded and rendered assistance to Kuok, helping lower him from the cliff face. Rangers received word of the accident at 4:40 p.m. and responded along with members of the Joshua Tree Search and Rescue (JOSAR) team. Kuok was treated by emergency personnel for back pain, rib injuries, and other possible internal injuries. (Source: From a Report by Joe Zarki, Public Information Officer, NPS Morning Report and from a posting on SuperTopo)

(Editor's Note: We do not get reports from JTNP on a regular basis. Thousands of climbers visit this famous climbing mecca every year. Fatalities have been rare. Accidents resulting in injuries are usually managed by the climbers on their own, as most falls are on one-pitch or less routes.)

STRANDED – BENIGHTED, EXPOSURE – INADEQUATE CLOTHING AND EQUIPMENT, LATE START
California, Yosemite Valley, Lost Arrow Spire

On April 13, Steve (45), Will (23), and Brent (22) set out to climb the classic Lost Arrow Spire (two pitches, 5.8/5.10 A2). Steve had climbed at least 15 big walls in the park over 30 years, as well as five previous trips up the Spire. Will and Brent were good free climbers, mostly on short routes, but they were new to the park and eager to try aid climbing for the first time, so Steve decided the Spire would be a good introduction, as the climbing is straight forward, the is exposure huge and immediate, and the exit by Tyrolean is a lot of fun. He first spent a day teaching them the basics of jumaring and climbing with étriers on short Valley problems, which they handled competently and safely.

The forecast on the morning of the 12th looked good, so the next day they started up the Yosemite Falls Trail at dawn carrying big packs. They took their time, broke for lunch at the top of the Falls, and arrived at the climb sometime around noon, though no one had a watch or cellphone, so they were estimating the hour.

The climb starts with a 250-300-foot rappel from the Valley rim into the bottom of the notch separating the main wall from the Spire. Parties typically tie two ropes together, anchor one end on the rim, and pass the knot on rappel. From the notch, two pitches of free and aid climbing wind up and left around the Spire to its tip, leaving the climbers separated from the Valley rim by a 140-foot gap. The pitches are led on a third rope while someone in the party drags the lower end of the rappel ropes along. Once on the Arrow Tip the rappel ropes, still anchored to the rim, can be rigged for a Tyrolean traverse from the Tip back to the rim.

From past experiences, Steve figured the climb would take four to five hours rim-to-rim. Dusk was about 2000, leaving them a three-hour cushion. At the worst they might have to hike back to the Valley in the dark.

As predicted, the weather was warm and sunny, so with no worries about time, they decided to leave most of their food and water, two of their three headlamps, and their warm jackets and long-underwear on the rim. For the climb they had two quarts of water, one Power Bar to split three ways, one headlamp, cotton long-sleeve-shirts or T-shirts, and light, un-insulated jackets. They had intended to bring a pair of ascenders for each person, but Will and Brent had to borrow all their aid gear on short notice and they somehow wound up one pair short. By the time Steve realized this, they were halfway up the trail, but he figured they could share ascenders since one person would always be leading.

They rappelled into the notch on two 200-foot ropes, passing the knot. By now it was early to mid-afternoon. The climb was Brent's and Will's to lead, so Brent took the first pitch, leading on their third rope, and had no problems. When he reached a small ledge 30 feet below the regular belay at Salathé Ledge, he asked if he should stop there. Thinking Brent was at Salathé Ledge, Steve said that would be fine.

Will led the next pitch, about 140 feet to the Arrow Tip. As he took off, Steve advised him that the pitch was notorious for rope-drag and that he could stop at an intermediate belay halfway up the pitch if drag became a problem. (The topo says, "Belay here if free climbing or too much rope drag.") Will completed the 30 feet up to Salathé Ledge and traversed left on aid. He found himself short of gear in places, which forced him to back-clean, i.e., to pull protection behind him for use ahead. When he reached the optional belay, the drag was manageable so Steve suggested he continue. But the drag soon became so bad that Will had to squat in his étriérs every five feet to pull the rope up. It was too late to stop then so he fought the drag all the way to the top. Communications were terrible from the noise of Yosemite Falls and from being around the corner from each other.

With all the back-cleaning and friction, the pitch took roughly three hours. This was much longer than Steve had planned and it put them far behind schedule. Will anchored the lead rope and the rappel rope (which he had dragged along) to bolts on the summit and Steve cleaned the pitch. When he joined Will, he could still easily see details at the anchor on the rim, but the sun had set and the light was fading fast. He was concerned that Will and Brent would be trying the Tyrolean crossing for the first time, as they hadn't practiced in the Valley. He didn't want them having a problem halfway across in the dark, so he decided that the safest option would be to rappel into the notch and jumar back up to the rim.

Steve rappelled on the fixed lead rope then Brent jumared up to Will to get his chance to stand on the Tip. He and Will joined the lead and rappel ropes so that they could rappel on both and retrieve them. Then Will rappelled, but they had misjudged the distance, and because the rappel rope hung in an arc between the Arrow Tip and the anchor on the rim, he found himself suspended by his ATC at the bottom of the arc. After several minutes of struggle, he managed to free the rappel rope from his ATC and descend only on the lead line. During this time he faced a 30-foot fall if the knot joining the ropes pulled through the anchor above.

Brent rappelled next and avoided Will's problem by stopping at Salathé Ledge, 30 feet above his partners. They had not sufficiently tested the rappel before he descended and when they tried to pull the ropes, they barely moved. Being closest to the summit, Brent had to jumar up again to see what was wrong. This time they managed to secure the rappel line so that Brent could ascend the lead line safely without depending on the joining knot above. By now it was completely dark. Brent had been searching his pockets for their lone headlamp, but had come up empty, so everything they did from here on was by feel and memory.

After Brent re-rigged the ropes on the Tip and rappelled again, he was able to pull the ropes down, but only by putting all his weight into it and screaming at the rope, pissed at all the little things going wrong. Then he rappelled again, just 30 feet on the lead line, from Salathé Ledge to Steve and Will. When they pulled the rope this time, it somehow looped over a flake above them in the dark. Without a light, they decided it was too risky to climb up to Salathé Ledge to free the rope, so Steve elected to pull one end and hope for the best. He retrieved about 90 feet before it became solidly jammed, but that was enough to tie it off, let everyone rappel into the notch, abandon the rope, and crawl over to a safe spot in the dark. They had long ago run out of water and it was getting cold, but finally, they thought, their problems were over. They would jumar up their fixed lines, be on the rim by 0200 or so, and walk down to the Valley.

Steve decided he would go up first and then lower their pack with his ascenders, food and water, headlamps, and warm clothes so that Will and Brent would have a safer and more comfortable ascent. If they hadn't lost the lead rope, Will and Brent could have used it to control the pack as Steve lowered it, but that was not an option now so they would have to risk the pack getting snagged.

Instead of the expected 20 minutes, it took Steve an hour or two to reach the rim. He had to be extremely careful with his rigging in the dark, double-checking his locking biners and safety slings. At one point he discovered he was attached to only one ascender. By the time he topped out, he was exhausted, his calves were cramping, and he was vomiting, probably from lack of food and water. He pulled up the ropes and tied on the pack so that it would reach the notch. He tried to lower it but it hung up, so he pulled it up and threw it out as far as he could. It snagged again. He knew he should descend to free it but he was exhausted, so he decided to bivy. In the morning he tried again, with the same result, but this time the rope was stuck in some way that prevented him from pulling it up at all. So tight, in fact, that he couldn't even attach his rappel device.

Meanwhile, Will and Brent had huddled together in the rocks. They wrapped their one flannel jacket around both of them and shivered and tried to sleep while they waited. Finally they heard what they figured was the pack come down and stop above them in the dark. It was too dangerous to try to retrieve it and they realized that even though they still had one pair of ascenders and could have initially sent a second person up to help Steve, they were completely dependant on him now. Sometime during the night, Brent discovered that his headlamp had been in his pocket the whole time, hidden under his leg loop. It was a bit late to be useful by that time.

At dawn Will and Brent could see the pack and loops of rope snagged 100 feet above them. The rope end was within their reach but with all the slack above liable to come loose, there was no safe way to ascend to the pack. They were screaming and yelling, "Rappel down the rope," hoping Steve would come down and free the pack. He could hear but not understand them and he was too exhausted to help any more. He slowly hiked out for help and eventually ran into someone on the trail with a cellphone.

The sun came out for a while and Will and Brent began to warm up, but they had no idea what was happening on their behalf, so they began yelling for help. The park switchboard lit up simultaneously with Steve's call and local residents reporting screams from the Arrow. Around 0900, Will and Brent heard a loudspeaker in the Valley letting them know a rescue team was on the way. Then it clouded up again, turned cold, and sprinkled and snowed on them just enough to get them damp. When the team reached the rim three hours later, all the rescuers were bundled up. Will said later, "It was a good warning. If you're more than one pitch off the ground, you've got to have rain gear." A rescuer reached them at 1330 and after some food and water, they were able to jumar to the rim under their own power. It wasn't easy. Brent's hands were cramping from the cold and Will was so exhausted from shivering all night he had to urged himself upward, "OK, I need to make it up to that next ledge..." It took Steve 48 hours of food, water, and rest to feel decent. Regarding the turn in the weather, Brent said, later, "We would have died there the next night. 100%."

Analysis

Steve may have been complacent because he'd climbed the Arrow five times before with no hassles, though he'd never rappelled from the tip. The big lesson should be obvious: Take your kit with you, including lots of food and water, a headlamp for each climber, and at least minimum warm clothes for a cold night. Without headlamps, they were at great risk for an accident as they tried to escape in the dark. A slight turn in the weather might have finished them off as well. In the end, everything depended on Steve and he was too exhausted to go down and free the pack. (Source: Steve, Will, Brent, and John Dill, NPS Ranger, Yosemite National Park)

(Editor's Note: In October 1984, a party of two reached the top of the Arrow at dark. Being inexperienced, they decided they should wait for morning to cross their Tyrolean. They weren't prepared for the breeze and mist from the falls and by dawn, one was dead of hypothermia. Read the details in ANAM 1985.)

FALL ON ROCK – SHORT FIXING WITHOUT A SELF-BELAY, INADEQUATE PROTECTION – FAILURE TO TEST AID PLACEMENT
California, Yosemite Valley, El Capitan.

On June 26, Degan (38) and Beth (32) were attempting a one-day climb of the Nose of El Capitan (Grade VI 5.9 C2). They had both climbed the Nose before and had extensive experience on Yosemite's big walls. They carried one 60-meter rope.

They approached the Nose via the Pine Line and started climbing the first pitch at 5:15 a.m. with Beth leading. The first pitch ends at a ledge and a two-bolt belay station. When she arrived, she pulled up all the slack rope, approximately 60 feet, and anchored the rope 60 feet from her end so that she could begin leading the next pitch with the slack while Degan cleaned the first pitch, thus saving time. When Degan reached the anchor he would start belaying her with the full rope.

Instead of rigging a self-belay, Beth proceeded to lead the second pitch tied only to her end of the rope with a 60-foot loop of slack stacked on the ledge. She free climbed the first 30 feet, a 5.7 left-facing corner that trended right, and then switched to aid climbing when the free climbing became 5.10. She was about 35 feet over the ledge when she placed her first piece on aid, a small offset Alien into a flared pin scar. She hand-tested the piece, then clipped in one of her aiders and stood up in it. As she fully weighted the piece, she heard it pop and she began falling down the slab.

Because of the slack in her system, Beth fell approximately 30 feet. A Camalot placed a few feet before she started aid climbing stopped her fall. She stopped approximately even with the top of pitch one, but on the slab to the right of the belay ledge. Based on her injuries, it appears that after initially falling on the slab above the belay anchor, she may have become caught in her rope, causing her to pendulum into the corner of the second pitch. Beth and Degan believe she sustained most of her injuries from the impact with this corner.

Degan could not see Beth fall and was not aware of the accident until he had almost arrived at the belay ledge and saw her hanging from the rope, upside down. He called to her but she did not respond. He heard her making gurgling noises. Degan continued ascending to the belay stance. He fixed himself to the anchor using his end of the rope with about ten feet of slack. Using this line, he was able to swing out to the right and reach Beth on the slab. He righted her, and she started to regain consciousness. He then tensioned back to the anchor with her, which provided some slack in her end of the lead line and allowed her to stand on the belay ledge (supported by Degan) without weighting the rope.

After securing Beth into the belay anchor, Degan, who is a Medic, assessed her injuries. She was not oriented to her location or what happened before the fall, but she seemed capable of following instructions and was sufficiently coordinated to assist in her own evacuation.

Degan could see a major avulsion injury of her right arm with some bone exposed, which she was guarding, and lacerations on her face including a laceration on her nose down to the bone, but the obvious concussion and her disorientation most concerned him. Degan called the park service about 6:00 a.m. and reported the accident and Beth's condition. Worried that she could deteriorate quickly, he began a self-evacuation knowing that an NPS rescue team was mobilized and would arrive at the base soon.

The first pitch is approximately 140 feet long and Degan had only one 200-foot rope, so he decided to lower Beth to the large ledge at the bottom of the first pitch. She was alert enough that she was following his instructions. He pulled the lead line down from pitch two through the protection that Beth had left on the pitch and tied her back into the rope.

Next he lowered her to the large ledge and instructed her to sit down. Once she was sitting, he instructed her to untie. The ledge is 6' x 6' and has 30 feet of third class terrain below. He was confident that she would stay seated. He then pulled Beth's end of the rope back up and made two rappels to reach her, using a single bolt in the middle of the pitch for the second rappel. Then he built an anchor, fixed the rope to it and was able rappel with Beth on a single line to reach ground level.

As he was completing these rappels around 6:20 a.m., Rangers Jack Hoeflich and Matt Stark arrived with medical gear and began stabilizing Beth for transport. The NPS litter team arrived soon after and carried Beth to an air ambulance at El Capitan Meadow. She was flown to Modesto and reached the emergency room approximately two hours after the fall.

In addition to suffering a concussion, Beth had a broken orbital floor in her skull, a lacerated and broken nose, other facial lacerations requiring stitches, de-gloving of the skin on the right arm, which after being repaired in surgery, resulted in a eight-inch scar on the forearm, two broken metatarsals in her right foot, a large rope burn on the right thigh, and significant bruising from the rope on the back of the right leg.

Analysis

After the accident, Beth stated that she could have switched to aid sooner, before the pin scars, in order to be standing in aiders on a solid placement while she tested it.

Short fix with a self-belay: If Beth had rigged a self-belay, she would have eliminated the slack and fallen only a few feet with no serious repercussions. "It was my choice not to tie in short," Beth said later. "I'd climbed the pitch so many times with out any problems that I didn't even think about it. Normally I wouldn't have pulled up so much slack rope but I thought I would be on belay by the time I finished the 5.7. I should have waited for Degan to belay me before starting the aid section."

The self-rescue dilemma: As a Medic, Degan had to decide whether to move Beth immediately in case she developed life-threatening intracranial bleeding or to wait for the SAR team while stabilizing her neck in case of a cervical spine injury. This dilemma is typical of off-road medicine and must often be addressed with minimal information.

Two ropes instead of one: Although Degan and Beth were able to self-evacuate fairly easily, carrying only one rope was a potentially risky decision. With only one rope, it may be impossible to escape a belay and secure an injured party. In addition, a retreat from high on the route, injury or not, is much more difficult, including, time and gear consumption. The Nose, like many routes on El Capitan, can be descended with two 60-meter ropes using fixed anchors without leaving gear.

Helmet: The foam on the inside of Beth's helmet was crushed and likely saved her from a more serious head injury. (Source: Degan and Beth, and Jesse McGahey, NPS Ranger, Yosemite National Park)

FALL ON ROCK, INADEQUATE PROTECTION, NO HARD HAT
California, Tuolumne Meadows, Cathedral Peak

On July 1 Shannon (29) and Margie (28) climbed part of Matthes Crest and decided to finish the day with an ascent of the Southeast Buttress of Cathedral Peak (five pitches of 5.6). This was their first day of climbing together, but both had climbed the route previously and knew it was well within their abilities (trad 5.10 and 5.9 respectively). Since it was four hours before dark and Shannon was the faster climber, they decided she would lead the whole climb. They wanted to bypass the 4th pitch chimney because neither of them liked chimneys, so Margie suggested staying left on an easy and protectable 5.4 variation that she had led previously. They carried the light alpine rack they had used that morning and simul-climbed 30 meters apart on a 60m x 8.1mm rope doubled to act as a twin (clipping both strands through all protection). Margie was wearing a helmet but Shannon was not.

Margie: Shannon climbed fast. We flew past the first belay station, and she belayed me to the top of the second pitch, where I returned the protection she had placed. We continued up until Shannon was out of sight above me, probably bypassing the chimney. The amount of slack between us was perfect, just a small smile in the rope. I was reaching out to clean the sling on a fixed piton when I heard, "Falling!" I grabbed the sling and braced myself with one hand and with the other I started jamming cams into a crack next to my head and clipped in my daisy. But the rope never came tight. The slack was gone but there was no force.

"Shannon!" I called. No response. I finished my anchor in case she fell further. Were her ropes intact? Would she start thrashing and roll off of whatever ledge had clearly stopped her fall? Was she even alive? I did not know how to safely get to her. I thought my only option was to climb while tied in to the rope — essentially soloing with her rope and her body as a backup, and with no idea what protection she had placed, but I was afraid that I might somehow pull her off the ledge. Otherwise I would have to wait where I was for help to come and not be able to care for her.

"Shannon!" I called two more times. No response. Then I heard "Shannon!" back, in an unfamiliar woman's voice at the base of the chimney pitch about 60 feet above and right of me.

"Can you see my friend? Can you please help us?" I called. "She fell. Do you have a cellphone?" replied the other climber. I had already reached for the phone and was turning it on. "I'm calling 911. Please have your climber lower to you and go to my friend," I said.

"I'm Ingrid. Max is climbing. I'll get him down," the voice answered. I was unable to see Shannon, Ingrid, or Max.

Ingrid had not known anyone else was on Cathedral, so she was surprised to see Shannon climb quickly by and out of sight. Then she heard, "Falling!" and briefly saw Shannon airborne; then she heard a "thud" on the ledges 30 feet to her left. She called out, "Are you OK?" but got no response, then she heard Margie calling. For about five minutes Shannon just moaned. Then she began screaming, "I'm going to die! Somebody help me!" but she never directly acknowledged Ingrid's voice, and Ingrid couldn't see her.

Margie: Shannon started screaming these high-pitched animal-like yelps. All I could think of was severe brain injury. She was alive, but I did not think she would survive. 911 connected me to Katie, a dispatcher in the park. "Is this an emergency?" she asked. "I have a fallen climber on Cathedral Peak, near the 4th pitch," I said. "She fell far. She is not conscious, but she is screaming. Please help." Katie immediately radioed my report to the park helicopter crew and the rangers in Tuolumne Meadows and then started asking me questions.

Meanwhile, Max was nearing the top of the chimney pitch. He and Ingrid could barely hear each other, so she was in a quandary. As a Wilderness First Responder (WFR), she wanted to immediately self-belay over to Shannon to see how she could help, but she couldn't take Max off belay until he was safe. She began tugging on the rope to get his attention. After a few minutes, they were able to talk and he fashioned an acceptable anchor. She decided to lower him so they could work as a team. This took two separate lowers with an intermediate anchor and much time, so when he finally reached Ingrid, she had him traverse straight to Shannon rather than take the time to re-rig and go over herself. Max got to Shannon 15-20 minutes after her fall and Ingrid kept him on belay thereafter.

Margie was also a WFR. Katie, the dispatcher, was an EMT, and Max had Basic First Aid. He could not see or hear Margie, 60 feet below, but Ingrid was able to hear both of them and to act as a relay. She said, later, "While Margie and Katie talked on the phone, I was able to give Max initial instructions, and when Margie or Katie had orders or questions, Max and I could provide the answers. We were able to work as a cohesive unit instead of being fragmented and emotional."

Shannon was lying on a ledge with her rope running through protection 20 feet above her and then down to Margie. She had cuts and scrapes all over her body. Her head was covered in blood and she was bleeding from her nose and mouth. Katie reminded Kathy to check Shannon's breathing. "Irregular," Max reported, "Oh wait, she's shivering, that's why." So he covered her with his own shirts and an emergency blanket he hauled up from Margie. "At one point she tried to sit up," Max said. "She started screaming and reached for her back, so I assumed she had a neck or back injury. I got her down and tried to stabilize her between my arms so that she couldn't move her neck or wiggle around and worsen her situation. I stabilized her the entire time, unless I was told to do something else. Katie asked us to set an anchor for the incoming rescuer, which I was able to do using gear from Shannon's rack."

About 45 minutes after her fall, the park helicopter located Shannon's party. Flying conditions permitted a safe hover over the ledge, so they decided to insert Jason, a ranger/medic, by short-haul. They landed in a meadow below to prepare the helicopter.

Margie: Katie asked me if there was anyone under Shannon, since a helicopter close to rock is dangerous. "I am," I said, "Is that OK?" Katie replied, "Anytime a helicopter flies in, there is risk of things getting blown around." I called up to Ingrid, "I need to get out from under Shannon for the rescue. Have Max put me on belay." But the helicopter was on its way and we suddenly felt really rushed. I climbed to Max and traversed to Ingrid. I could barely see Shannon under the silver blanket as I went by. The medic was coming in, hanging on the line under the helicopter. He motioned to Max to stay with Shannon."

Jason landed on the ledge, clipped in, and the helicopter left. Shannon was scared, confused, combative, and crying over and over, "You're killing me!" and "Am I going to die?" She fought the whole time, trying to rip off the cervical collar they applied, so Jason and Max packaged her quickly in the litter as best they could and called back the aircraft. At Jason's signal, Max released the final sling anchoring the litter to the cliff. Jason and Shannon were lifted off and short-hauled to Tuolumne Meadows. Then Shannon was loaded aboard the helicopter and flown to the park heli-base where she was transferred to an air ambulance for the flight to Modesto.

Margie: When the helicopter left, it became completely silent. We were alone on the wall with ropes and gear everywhere and all of us were shaken up, wondering if we should try to lead out in our current mental state. With one good rope and three climbers, it would take forever, and dark was an hour away. But then a team of rescuers arrived at the base. They were Plan B, in case the helicopter hadn't been able to rescue Shannon. They yelled to us, offering to come up and help us rappel. It was a much-appreciated offer and the wisest option.

Shannon reached the trauma center three hours after her fall. Her most severe injuries were a compression fracture of T12 and a burst fracture of L1, but she had escaped any damage to her spinal cord. She also somehow avoided a serious brain injury, but not by much. She still only remembers walking to the start of the route, then nothing until the ER. After several months in a full-torso brace, she is fully healed and climbing again.

Analysis

It appears that Shannon was off route on a hard section that offered limited protection. This is surprising, considering that she indicated that she is a timid, though competent, leader. It is not known why she fell. No protection came out and all signs suggest she fell about 40 feet.

Protecting the pitch required tiny cams and nuts, but their light rack had nothing small. Simul-climbing may have played a part, since they weren't meeting frequently to discuss the route and to replenish Shannon's gear. Shannon now thinks that simul-climbing closer together would improve that situation, but it's hard to pin the accident on simul-climbing itself, since everything seemed to be going well. She and Margie both felt some pressure to climb fast given the late hour. This may have influenced Shannon to run out her pro or spend less time route finding, but that doesn't fit with her leading style and, in fact, they had plenty of time.

Shannon said, "This was the first day in my climbing experience that I hadn't worn a helmet," she recalled, "with the possible exception of a sport route. I remember, before the climb, wishing I had one." Margie said, "If I'd been out with my longtime climbing partner and she didn't have a helmet, I would have been very comfortable telling her, 'You're not a God. Wear your helmet!' but I didn't know Shannon that well, so I failed to raise the issue."

"It seemed like a miracle that Margie had a phone," Max said, and he was almost right. "I always climb with one," said Margie, "but that morning, five of us left the car in a rush for Matthes Crest and I realized it was still in the car. I didn't know everyone in the party well and was afraid they'd make fun of me, so I made some excuse about sunglasses and ran back for the phone. The helmet and the phone were good lessons. I should not be shy about raising safety concerns with new partners."

Cell coverage in the backcountry is sparse, but several high points can "see" a tower in the distance and the upper part of this climb is one of those. (See Yosemite, Marmot Dome, in this issue.) Even if a climb has no coverage and you have to go for help, you may get cell service long before reaching the car, so bring your phone. Be sure to tell your partners where the phone is, as you may be the patient.

Given the circumstances and the unknowns facing them, Ingrid and Max effectively carried out their plan to work as a team and their presence was a great stroke of luck for Shannon, Margie, and the rescue team. The on-scene help Margie, Ingrid, and Max were able to provide is also an example of why climbers should take some form of a wilderness first aid course. (Source: Shannon, Margie, Ingrid, and Max. Also Jason Ramsdell and John Dill, NPS Rangers, Yosemite National Park)

(Editor's Note: Shannon's injuries are not unusual and sometimes they are not obvious. In late August, Colin (29) and three friends climbed Cathedral Peak and started down the back side. Colin tried a steep shortcut while unroped and fell/ tumbled 60 feet, losing consciousness briefly. With his partners' help, he limped out three miles with an obvious wrist fracture, a fractured foot, and a seven-inch scalp wound, but the CT scan at the hospital also found three fractured cervical vertebrae. Incredibly, the neck fractures were stable.)

FALL ON ROCK – SLACK IN ROPE WHILE SIMUL-CLIMBING
California, Yosemite National Park, Commitment

On June 17, Floyd (47), an experienced climber, was with two partners, belaying them from above. They were simul-climbing and slack developed between them. One fell some distance, hitting a tree. He fractured his heel bone. (Source: John Dill, NPS Ranger, Yosemite National Park)

Analysis

This is a common problem with simul-climbing, which is why it is included here. (Source: Jed Williamson)

FALL ON ROCK, INADEQUATE PROTECTION
California, Yosemite National Park, El Capitan, The Nose

On June 26, Holly (32) and her partner Jeff were climbing the first pitch of The Nose when she took a 40-foot leader fall. She fractured her elbow and had abrasions. She was carried to the road and flown to the hospital. (Source: John Dill, NPS Ranger, Yosemite National Park)

Analysis

Falling on the first pitch is a common occurrence. Not having adequate protection in this situation is the reason climbers fall to the deck. (Source: Jed Williamson)

STRANDED, CLIMBING ALONE, INADEQUATE EQUIPMENT, NOT ON ANY KNOWN ROUTE
California, Yosemite National Park, Marmot Dome

Park dispatch received a cellphone call from climber Daniel Susman (20s) around 10 a.m. on July 15th, in which Susman reported that he'd become ledged-out while scrambling on a dome near Merced Lake and that he'd need assistance getting off the ledge. He said that he wasn't in any immediate danger but that he was unable to ascend or descend from his location. Upon flying past, rescue personnel were shocked to discover that Susman had downplayed his predicament. They found that he was standing on minuscule ledge, clinging to the rock on a nearly vertical wall approximately 800 feet above the valley floor.

Susman's position was deemed to be too tenuous to try to retrieve him directly by short haul. The concern was that the buffeting winds from the aircraft might dislodge Susman from his stance before he could be made secure. The pilot, Richard Shatto, and the two spotters, Jeff Pirog and Boots Davenport, had a difficult time maintaining a steady hover with the aircraft due to gusting winds. Ranger Keith Lober was short-hauled into a location 50 feet above Susman's perch, where he power drilled three anchor bolts. Ranger Eric Gabriel was then short-hauled to the anchor station. Lober lowered Gabriel down to Susman, who was then secured in a "screamer suit." He and Gabriel were then short-hauled off the face.

Analysis

Cellphone coverage in Yosemite backcountry is generally nonexistent. Susman was incredibly lucky, as the location where he became stuck was just high enough for the cell signal to peek over the surrounding rock faces and hit the Sentinel Dome repeater, the only repeater in that area of remote wilderness.

Susman had sustained and recovered from two short falls just before deciding to stop and request help. He was wearing hiking boots at the time. (Source: Keith Lober, Emergency Medical Services Program Manager)

(Editor's Note: This is another case of a scrambler ending up in a climbing situation. This individual had indeed come to Yosemite to do some climbing and had led climbs up to 5.10 prior to this. He is a member of a prominent college outing club in New England.)

FALL ON ROCK – OFF ROUTE, INADEQUATE PROTECTION, NO HELMET
California, Mono County, Inyo National Forest, Third Pillar of Dana

On August 30, Jeff Maurer (47) and Jo-Lynne DeNapoli (36) were planning on climbing the Regular Route of the Third Pillar of Mount Dana (Grade III 5.10b, six pitches). The climb is approached from Tioga Road just east of Yosemite National Park and is located in Mono County. After a three-mile hike to the Dana Plateau, climbers scramble about 700 feet down a third-class gully to the base of the rock formation.

Jeff and Jo-Lynne were both experienced climbing in the Sierra Nevada (Jeff over 20 years and Jo-Lynne ten years) and led up to traditional style 5.10 free climbing. They had not climbed a multi-pitch route together before, but were good friends and were confident in their abilities to climb the route. They carried a standard rack of gear and a 60-meter rope.

The following is Jo-Lynne's account of the accident:

"When we arrived at the base at 9-9:30 a.m., there was a party on the first pitch of the Regular Route and we had passed two more parties on the approach trail coming to climb the same route. So we decided to try an alternate crack system about 30 feet to the right of the Regular Route that we thought was Lenticular Limbo (Grade III 5.10c). After three pitches, this route joins the Regular Route. By the flip of a rock at the top of the plateau, Jeff had won the lead of the first pitch. Full of energy, he led up the initial corner. After about 30 feet, the crack split in two directions.

"Because we weren't sure which crack to follow, Jeff and I both checked our topos. I had a hand-drawn map copied from the Don Reid-Chris Falkenstein guidebook, *Rock Climbs of Tuolumne Meadows*, and Jeff had a page ripped out of the same guidebook as well as the description from R.J. Secor's *Peaks Passes and Trails*. We both concluded that we were not on Lenticular Limbo and didn't know what climb it was.

"I had a feeling that Jeff should come down and we should just climb the Regular Route, but I never voiced this opinion to him and still regret my silence. We did agree that once he got to the halfway mark of his rope, we would decide whether to keep climbing or retreat and climb the Regular Route.

"Jeff chose to go to the right crack system in a shallow dihedral. He yelled down that the climbing was low angle, implying that it was not too difficult. Soon after that, a few small golf-ball-sized rocks came down, so I moved to the right to get out of the fall zone. From this position I could no longer see Jeff climbing.

"All of a sudden Jeff said something. As I replay it in my head I think he said 'Whoa!' but it was not loud or concerned. I felt the rope go slack as if there was a fall and I quickly pulled in one arm-length of slack and held my brake hand down preparing to catch the fall.

"Jeff had placed five pieces of gear at that point, each about ten to 15 feet apart. I am guessing that he was about 50 feet up. As he fell, I felt the rope come tight and then 'pop' or release twice. I then saw his body rushing down in a fall line five to ten feet from me. I could hear the sound of him ripping through the air, but I don't remember hearing Jeff say anything as he came down. The rope did not come tight and Jeff hit the ground full force.

"I do not remember walking over to him. My first memory is looking at his face and seeing he was unconscious. I yelled for help and stabilized his head and neck and covered his head with my hands to try to stop the bleeding. At first I wanted to move him into a better position, since his head was below the rest of his body on the talus, but I was afraid of damaging his spinal cord if I tried to move him myself. At this point I tried to gently lift his head above his heart. As I moved him, I heard air move through his mouth and then a rattling sound from his lungs. I looked at his eyes and his pupils were dilated. I couldn't feel a pulse and did not observe any breathing.

"I didn't have a watch, but I'm guessing the sequence of events from the time that Jeff fell to my initial assessment lasted less than one minute. I continued to scream for help to the party on the Regular Route. They were around the corner and I could not see them. I remember wishing that they would have just fixed the line and descended as fast as possible, but they chose to do two rappels to come down to the base.

"Squatting, I continued cradling his head in my lap and I begged the team descending to help me and offered to replace any gear they needed to leave behind. Although in my head I knew Jeff was dead, my heart could not suppress the thought that with a little more care, he could still live. I also craved a second opinion so that the responsibility of his diagnosis was no longer on me. I continuously screamed for help as my legs cramped holding Jeff's head.

"When the climbers on the Regular Route, Joe Stock and Cathy Flanagan, arrived safely at the base, Joe felt for Jeff's pulse and confirmed that he was dead. Joe is not a doctor nor did he state having medical experience. Joe took some pictures at the scene, and I told him Jeff's name and that he worked for the National Park Service in Yosemite as a Wildlife Biologist.

"Joe ran for help and I sat with Cathy. She did her best to support me and I was grateful that I was not alone. We waited for what seemed like hours for help to come. Finally, I could see a helicopter flying in from the southeast. Shortly after it came into view, it turned around and flew back the same direction.

"I grew impatient with the waiting and was thankful that Jeff was not suffering and dying as we waited for help. In hindsight, I think that Jeff liked spending a little more time out in the mountains, but my fear was that he was still alive and that I was not caring enough for him. This, coupled with my own need for friends and comforting, was torturous.

"I did not want to leave Jeff alone, but by 6:00 p.m., it was getting cold and the possibility of a rescue that night was becoming less likely. I said goodbye to Jeff and we walked up the gully to the plateau and back to my car at the Tioga Lake trailhead.

"In the days that followed I wished I had had more of a ceremony for Jeff. Death is so removed from our being. So unexpected. The rock-climbing 'How to' series could use the 'How to deal when your partner dies'—poems and prayers and songs to sing as your friend passes from this world to the next. I felt trained for dealing with an injured partner, but not a dead one."

(NB: The next day, after another aircraft effort was cancelled due to wind, the Yosemite and Mono County teams raised Jeff's body 700 feet to the plateau and flew him out by helicopter.)

Analysis

Jeff and Jo-Lynne decided to head up an alternate crack system (thinking it was Lenticular Limbo), and from the ground they thought it didn't look that bad. It was later discovered that Jeff was climbing the first pitch of "The One That Almost Got Away," (5.10d/11a) a newer route not in the guide. The pitch looks easier and lower angle than it is and it abruptly gets more difficult with only sparse placements for "thin" and "dirty" protection.

The cracks in High Sierra granite, especially those that haven't seen much traffic, can be flaky, grainy, or fragile. If protection is marginal, climbers should assume it will fail.

A helmet may not have saved Jeff's life after a fall of 75 feet, but we know that helmets save lives and prevent or minimize injury from leader falls, seconding falls, and rockfall. (Source: Chris Simmons, Joe Stock, Jesse McGahey, NPS Ranger, Yosemite National Park—with special thanks to Jo-Lynne DeNapoli.)

FALLING ROCK — FALL ON ROCK
California, Sequoia and Kings Canyon National Parks, Mount Whitney

On October 3rd, two men were climbing the East Buttress route (5.7) on Mount Whitney. They were on a ledge at 13,500 feet when a large rock fell from above and hit one of them on the helmet and upper back. The impact pushed him down to the ledge and caused him to experience neck and back pain with numbness and tingling on his entire left side. The uninjured climber assisted his partner in rappelling down two rope-lengths, but his companion's pain was so intense that he could not continue.

A cellphone call was made to the park that came in around 10:00 p.m. On Sunday morning, the park's helicopter flew ranger/medics Deb Brenchley and Rich Browne in to locate the climbers and evaluate the possibility of a short-haul extraction. They were found at their camp at Iceberg Lake. Due to the cold, they had continued to descend in the dark and finally arrived at their camp at 5:00 a.m. The temperature when the rescue team arrived was -16° C (about 3° F). The injured climber was transported to Southern Inyo Hospital, where he was diagnosed as having suffered a fractured scapula, broken ribs, and a compression fracture of his c-spine. (Source: Michael Cole, Lodgepole Subdistrict Ranger)

FALL ON ROCK — HASTE, INADEQUATE PROTECTION
California, Yosemite Valley, Middle Cathedral Rock

On October 3, Jake Martin (29) and I (30) decided to climb Central Pillar of Frenzy (five pitches, 5.9) on Middle Cathedral Rock, something moderate and with a close approach that I had climbed a few times in the past. We climbed the first three pitches pretty quickly. I was leading the 4th pitch and remembered that you can rap from the top of the 5th (the typical end to the route) to the top of the 3rd, so I decided to lead the two pitches as one; I clipped the anchor at the top of 4 and continued up, placing gear periodically on easy terrain. I was pretty far above my last piece of gear and thought to place a piece in a good crack when I caught site of the anchors about 15 feet above. Since it was only 15 feet to the anchor, I kept climbing without placing gear, with the usual confidence that I would not fall. I was doing a few short, insecure, but relatively easy lie back moves with my eye on the anchor when my foot that was smeared on the smooth wall spontaneously blew.

I had a lot of time to think about my situation as I free-fell, and I realized that my last piece of gear was more than 50 feet below. I had time to yell, "Holy Shit!" take a breath, and resume yelling. Along the way I banged into the wall and began to slide down the near-vertical slab, and then I must have got caught up on something because I began to tumble over and over, wondering when the rope would catch.

At one point I was upside down and banging into the wall and then, when the rope started to catch, I flipped around and ultimately stopped, right-side up. I was wearing a helmet which, when later inspected, had multiple fresh dents and scratches and has thus been retired. Jake kept asking me whether I was OK, and I kept waving him off as I hung my head, trying to overcome the mental and physical shock and injuries of the fall. I was pretty delirious; my hands, elbows, and ankles were bleeding; I had ripped the pads off of a few fingers; and my ankle, wrist, and arm hurt.

After a few minutes, when I had regained enough sense to communicate,

I asked Jake to lower me ten feet to the anchor at the top of 4, not really knowing if there was enough rope. I had fallen from within ten feet of the top of five to ten feet above the top of 4, a total of 120 feet, according to the topo. As he lowered me, I was seeing stars and everything was swirling around me. At pitch 4, I was able to slump onto a sloping ledge, clip in to the anchor, untie, and with Jake's help from below, pull the rope through the gear above and back down to me, leaving three pieces of gear in pitch 5 above me. (No gear pulled when I fell.) Then Jake lowered me to his belay at the top of 3 and I cleaned the gear from pitch 4 on the way down. From 3 he was able to lower me down each pitch and then rappel himself, until we reached the ground.

I hobbled to the clinic and got all my wounds cleaned. We took bets on whether I had broken my arm, because there was a sub-dermal hematoma—a baseball-sized lump—on my forearm. It turned out I had no broken bones, but I had sprained my ankle and wrist and I needed stitches in my hand. As I write this, almost four weeks later, my ankle and the huge hematoma are still not healed, but I was extremely lucky. (Source: James Woods)

Analysis

Helmet. Jake: "If James had not been wearing his helmet, he would have experienced SEVERE head trauma—at several points during his fall, he tumbled backwards heels-over-head with his head the first thing impacting the rock."

James: "In the past I generally wore one for all aid climbs and most long trad lines, but not for sport climbing and cragging. At the base of the climb I asked Jake if he was going to wear a helmet and he replied, 'Yes, I always wear a helmet.' I said, 'I usually don't for cragging, but it's Middle Cathedral, so I will,' referring to the large amounts of rockfall we typically associate with Middle. After this experience I will not be leaving the ground without one!"

Haste. Jake: "We were climbing in the shade, and James had left his wind jacket at the base. The afternoon wind picked up and I had my jacket on at the top of pitch 3. I remember James saying something about getting the hell off this thing so we could lounge in the warm sun and drink beer in the meadow. In short, he was in a hurry to get off."

James: "The best point Jake made, paraphrased, is that if you push your luck long enough something's bound to happen eventually, but you never think it's going to happen to you. I had recently climbed the Nose in a Day and the Rostrum, long and difficult routes, so I was in a mentality to climb fast and not place much protection on easier sections, with the confidence that I would not fall. The end result was absolutely the scariest and most humbling experience in my life." (Source: James Woods, Jake Martin, and John Dill, NPS Ranger, Yosemite National Park)

FALL ON ROCK – BELAY FAILURE, NO STOPPER KNOT, DISTRACTION
California, Yosemite Valley, El Capitan

On October 8, Nicolas Lebaut (29) and Davina Borrow-Jones (32) were climbing at the base of the Southwest Face of El Capitan. Nicolas decided to lead Little John Left, a short, one-pitch, 5.8 route leading up and right to fixed rappel anchors. Davina did not feel like following, so they agreed he would simply lower Nicolas off and Nicolas would clean the pitch on the way down. They checked the height of the climb in their guidebook. It stated 80 feet and they had a 60m rope, which was plenty long enough for Nicolas's descent.

Nicolas climbed the route, placing protection along the way. Meanwhile, another party, Mike and Rachel, was descending the Heart Ledges rappel route on fixed ropes overhanging Little John Left. The two parties recognized each other and everyone began chatting.

Davina began lowering Nicolas. He had full control of the rope and a good view of Nicolas. Since the climb angles up and right, Nicolas had to pull himself to the left and partially down-climb to stay within reach of his protection as he descended. As he removed the lowest piece, he swung back to the right under the anchor above.

Details are incomplete from this point on, but apparently Davina was caught off guard by the surge of tension from Nicolas's weight. He had been standing at the start of the climb, so he was dragged to the right because of the angle of pull to the belay anchor above. The talus slopes steeply down to the right here, so as he moved right he also descended, significantly lengthening Nicolas's lowering distance. He also may have elected to scramble even further down the slope to move out of the other party's way. As he continued lowering Nicolas, he became distracted by Mike and Rachel's descent and apparently forgot to keep an eye on his end of the rope. The end must not have been anchored or knotted, because it suddenly passed through Davina's hand and through his belay device. Nicolas tumbled 20 feet to the talus and was immediately in agony from a back injury.

Rachel called 911. The first medic reached Nicolas about 20 minutes after his fall, followed by the evacuation team. They immobilized him and carried him down to El Capitan Meadow, where he was transferred to an air ambulance and flown to Modesto. At the trauma center he was diagnosed with compression fractures of L1 and L4. He wore a back brace for three months but has fully recovered.

Analysis
It is almost inevitable that plans will change and distraction will happen, so staying alert is essential. Looking around for common hazards such as sloping ground or a difference between lengths of ascent and descent are part of this.

The belayer should anchor if the stance is unstable. But the most important point is ALWAYS ANCHOR OR KNOT THE BELAY ROPE! Do this even on ridiculously short climbs to maintain the habit and to set a good example. (Source: John Dill, NPS Ranger, Yosemite National Park)

DARKNESS – STRANDED
California, Pinnacles National Monument, Condor Crag

On the evening of November 15th, park staff assisted two climbers down from a climbing route after they had become stranded due to nightfall. Both climbers were uninjured.

The climbers were able to place a cellphone call to a friend around 6:00 p.m. after they could no longer climb in darkness. They were near the top of a 500-foot route on the Condor Crag formation in the High Peaks area of the park. They were in different locations on the route and could not complete the final 100 feet without additional light. Rangers contacted the party via cellphone and determined their location and condition before the phone battery was exhausted. With an overnight forecast of 25 degrees F and gusting winds, rangers and search and rescue team members were dispatched to climb to their location. The crew of a California Highway Patrol helicopter located the pair using infrared radar and a powerful "Night Sun" floodlight. Assisted by monument staff, the climbers then completed the route and descent. By the time they got down at 1:00 a.m., they'd been on the route for 14 hours. (Source: Brett Hergert, Operations Supervisor)
(Editor's Note: In the not too distant past, these climbers would have spent a night out—and maybe worse. Cellphones and the technical equipment available to rescue personnel have changed the game of climbing considerably. Maybe we should revive the notion of creating no-rescue zones…)

FALL ON ROCK, GEAR SLING CAUGHT ON CAM DURING FALL – STRANGULATING CLIMBER
California, Kings Canyon National Park, Obelisk

My name is Patrick Callery. Our friend David Shirley and I were climbing with Ishun Chan on the South Face route of the Obelisk when she was tragically killed on November 8. This report of the accident is provided with the hopeful intent to provide some answers for her many friends and loved ones and with the hope that her tragic passing may in some way better inform the climbing community of potential dangers in our sport.

Sometime in early October I pitched Ishun on a trip to the Obelisk. A classic backcountry rock with an arduous approach, the Obelisk had been on my to-do list for years, and Ishun was enthusiastic about joining me for it. We half expected we'd eventually cancel the trip plan given the lateness of the season, but continued fair and mild mountain weather throughout late October kept the window of opportunity open. As the weekend approached, David also joined in. We grew a little apprehensive about the forecast for cold temperatures, but it would be only marginally colder than we had comfortably dealt with on Charlotte Dome two weeks prior, and the weather was forecast to remain stable throughout the weekend and several days past. Out of the many fine routes on the peak, we chose the South Face as our objective given its comparatively low rating (5.6 per Secor and Vernon guides), fewer anticipated pitches, and sunny exposure. We knew it would be a long day and anticipated hiking out Sunday night in the dark, as we had done on the Charlotte Dome trip.

The next morning, we rose at 5:30 a.m. and started hiking at 6:00 a.m. We made good time on the approach and arrived at the saddle northeast of the Obelisk around 7:15 a.m. We took our time changing shoes and gearing up, and found the approach down the east side of the Obelisk more tedious with bushes than expected. After poking around the base of the South Face and studying the topos and other route beta, we settled on the most obvious "vegetated gully" that appears at the base of the South Face route. Entering the gully appeared tricky and awkward, so I offered to lead a pitch on the face to the left and traversed in to the gully about 100 feet up. Ishun followed, and we belayed David up from the proper gully entrance to save time. Above here, the gully appeared easy and we unroped to climb the next 150-200 feet solo. We continually discussed whether we were really in the proper South Face "long, broken chimney" or rather the "recess" mentioned in the Vernon guide. Much of this part of the gully was fourth-class, with a few steep and awkward stemming/chimney moves to get around chock stones and bulges. Upon reaching a particularly difficult bulge, we opted to rope up and continue climbing. It was now a little after 9:00 a.m. Our intent was to top out by noon so as to get a good start on the pack out before nightfall.

Ishun took the next lead, starting up and over a steep bulge that she adamantly noted was somewhat stiffer than 5.6. Yet another bulge higher up was similarly difficult, but also cleared in good style. About 70 feet up, the gully ended in a steep wall. She found an awkward exit to the right, climbing out of our sight, though we had excellent voice communication here and she relayed some of what she saw. The steep face directly above the top of the gully looked intimidating and she thought she might traverse right to see what lay above. She was starting to move a little more slowly now and I remember continually looking down at my watch, concerned about our pace. It was now about 9:45 a.m. I shouted from below that if things didn't look right, she should put in an anchor and bring us up to discuss our options. She proceeded a little farther and I hollered out that she had reached the halfway mark on the rope. She responded that she would climb another

10-20 feet and anchor. After a couple minutes, I heard the terrible scraping noise of a steep slab fall and the rope fluttered as Ishun cried out.

Surprisingly, the rope did not come taut. In this brief moment I rationalized that she had either caught her fall or stopped on a ledge. David and I called up to see if she was OK. There was no reply. We shouted a few more times and heard nothing. Moving quickly, I pulled the rope tight, locked off the belay, and backed it up. We fixed a Klemheist to the rope and reinforced the anchor for upward pull, then tied off the rope to the anchor and stepped out of the belay. About half the rope was out, so we reasoned I could reach her on the other half. We also had a single twin-rope (for the third climber) and I tied this to my harness to trail up. David put me on belay and I proceeded on the free half of the lead rope, clipping the pieces Ishun had placed on lead. The climbing was difficult as she had said and my heart was racing. I tried to climb quickly but deliberately. Eventually I reached the top of the gully and could see Ishun to my right.

At the top of the gully, she had exited right and climbed up and right over steep slabs about ten feet to a tied-off knob. Much of this face was very modestly featured, and conspicuously lacking the copious chickenheads we had found on the first pitch far below. She was now resting about 20 feet to the right and slightly down from this last piece. She was oriented vertically with her back to me and I could see a piece fixed to the rock directly above her. One arm was thrust upward and she was leaning against the wall. I continued to call out to her in as calm a voice as I could muster, trying to reassure her (and myself) that everything was going to be OK. I climbed up to clip the top piece, then down-climbed and proceeded to traverse out to her on steep and surprisingly blank friction, with a few small footholds for balance. As I got to within ten feet of her, David called out from below that I was now out of rope. I'd misjudged the rope length and now couldn't reach her. I inched back to the left to more secure footholds, tied into the haul line, climbed back up to the high knob and clipped it. After David put me on belay with the haul line, I untied from the lead rope and traversed back out. It's hard to remember exactly, but by this point at least 30 minutes had passed since the fall.

When I reached Ishun, I could see her gear sling was pulled tight under one shoulder and around the other side of her neck. The gear sling itself was hanging from a single cam, the trigger bar having caught and held on a small knob directly above her head. This is what had stopped her fall without loading the rope. There was a loose runner clipped to the rope, indicating she may have been trying to sling a knob when she fell. She did not appear to be breathing and I wasn't sure if I was detecting a faint carotid pulse. There were red trauma marks on her neck and thin white foam at her lips.

I was horrified to find that I could not release the gear sling, as it was holding her entire body weight. We were 20 feet out on a pendulum exposure and I could not find sufficient footholds to apply enough leverage to pull off the sling or to lift the cam from the protrusion above. The surface features available (a few small, rounded knobs in inconvenient locations) presented only very marginal protection between our position and the last good piece. What followed was almost mechanical. Somehow I was able to rig a lowering system near the previous good piece and release Ishun from her position without causing a further pendulum swing. I am wracked with doubts as to whether I made all the right decisions in administering emergency care while managing the anchoring in our precarious position. All I wanted was to get her off the rock safely and see her wake up. I tried to hold out high hopes throughout the ordeal, but deep in my heart I think I knew she was already gone.

(Editor's Note: A long description of the down-climbing and extrication and followed. Mr. Callery offered the following, which will serve as the analysis.)

First, Ishun [was] an excellent climber and quite experienced leading on backcountry trad routes. She [had] a solid understanding of protection and anchor dynamics and is a careful route finder. She [was] an exceptionally strong climber and share[d] my unhealthy enjoyment of suffering heavy packs over long approaches to reach remote backcountry gems. She had many long backcountry routes under her belt, most recently a two-day outing to climb the South Face of Charlotte Dome, which we successfully completed in good style two weeks prior to the accident. She [had] demonstrated very solid capability leading sustained 5.8 trad routes, with raw technical ability well into the 5.10 range. I would like to emphasize my opinion that this accident was not a result of inexperience or exceeding abilities.

It appears she may have simply slipped and come off her stance, perhaps while trying to place protection. She should have taken a swinging pendulum fall on the steep slab, with the likely consequence some scraped limbs, a possible bonk on her (helmeted) head, and at worst maybe a sprained ankle. The cam catching on a small knob and stopping her fall was an extremely unlikely occurrence with a devastating outcome.

(Editor's Note: This report was edited from a posting by Patrick Callery on SuperTopo and SummitPost. Climbing Web sites often have deeply personal postings such as this one. We appreciate the candor and specifics provided, even though not all the details we seek are embedded.)

STRANDED CLIMBER, EXCEEDING ABILITIES, INADEQUATE CLOTHING, EQUIPMENT AND FOOD AND CLIMBING UNROPED
Colorado, Rocky Mountain National Park, Lumpy Ridge

A party of three (two males, early 20s, and one female, 17) began soloing Organ Pipes (5.6) on the Twin Owls formation, Lumpy Ridge on January

16th late in the day. All three had little or no climbing experience. They only had lightweight cotton clothes and no food to spend the night. One of the males made it safely to the top of the route. The other one stopped after about 30 feet and was able to down-climb to the base of the route. However, the female climber stopped about 20 feet below the top of the route. She could not climb up or down. One of the other members of the party called 911 around 1730.

An NPS team responded to the climbers and lowered one of the team members to the stranded climber about 1900. He secured her to a rope and helped dress her in warmer clothing. The rest of the NPS team then lowered both the stranded climber and the NPS person to the ground. They hiked out and reached the trailhead at 2145.

Analysis

This party underestimated the difficulty of the intended route and over estimated their climbing abilities. They climbed past the point where they could have safely down-climbed to the base.

Fortunately, this group was a party of three and two of them made it off the route. If they had not called for help, it is unlikely that the stranded climber would have returned uninjured. By the time rescuers reached her she could not move her lower legs and could barely hold onto the rock anymore.

Honest and continued assessment of one's skills, open communication between the party members, proper equipment, and training can prevent incidents like this. Many times when climbing teams fail to talk openly with one another, they end up in situations like this where one member is well within his/her comfort zone and another member is well outside of his/hers. Communication about the intended route and the skills of the climbers in the party will often reveal discrepancies long before more serious situations arise. (Source: Edited from a report by Mark Pita, Search & Rescue Program Manager, Rocky Mountain National Park)

RAPPEL ERROR – THREADED ROPES INCORRECTLY, FALL ON ROCK
Colorado, Garden of the Gods, Red Twin Spire

During the afternoon on February 7, a climber (21) fell over 50 feet sustaining serious life-threatening injuries. He had just climbed the popular route Potholes, a moderate 5.8 route up the steep east face of Red Twin Spire in the Gateway area. The 55-foot-high route, protected by four fixed pitons and bolts, works up a series of potholes to an airy exit and a small summit the size of a dining room table. At the edge of the summit is an anchor composed of fixed pitons linked together with chain for top-roping, lowering, and rappelling.

The climber apparently untied, threaded his rope through a large quick-link on the chains, and prepared to rappel with a figure-8 descender. He failed, however, to thread both sides of his rope through the descender and locking carabiner, instead just securing one side in the device. So when he stood up and weighted the rope, it zipped through the quick-link and dropped him down the vertical face to a concrete sidewalk, which surrounds Red Twin Spire and neighboring White Twin Spire. The Colorado Springs Fire Department high-angle rescue team responded and evacuated the climber. (Source: About.com website - http://climbing.about.com)

RAPPELLING ERROR – UNEVEN ROPES, HASTE
Colorado, Ouray Ice Park, New Frontier

A climber rappelled off the end of his rope on February 17. He explained that he was in a rush. He set up an anchor, clipped the rope to the middle mark, threw the rope, started rapping, and suddenly found himself falling/ tumbling. He mistook the 15-foot mark for the middle mark of the rope. Luckily he was at New Frontier, so he only fell approximately 30 feet. Had it been elsewhere, the fall would have been much, much worse. He suffered only a broken ankle and wrist.

Analysis

A few tips to rappel safely: Know your rope's midpoint, tie bulky knots in both ends of the rope to jam in your rappel device; use a backup such as a autoblock, prusik, or kleimheist knot on the rope; clip to your harness with a locking carabiner, have your partner double-check all systems, and finally, visually check that the rope ends reach the next station or the ground before you rappel (Source: Edited from a report on rockclimbing.com posted on 2/18/09)

FALL ON ROCK, ROPE PULLED THROUGH BELAY DEVICE
Colorado, Clear Creek Canyon, Wall of the 90's

On March 10, I (36) had successfully climbed the route Hot Stuff (5.10c). My two partners and I were climbing on a 70m rope, a standard length for this route. I was being lowered when the rope went through the belayer's device resulting in my dropping about 20 feet to the belay ledge. I then bounced off the ledge, fell an additional 20 feet, and tumbled farther down the scree. Injuries included a lacerated ear, abrasions, and a concussion. *(Editor's Note: A cellphone was used to report the incident to rescue personnel.)*

Analysis

The simple solution for preventing this accident would have been to tie a knot in the end of the rope on the belayer's end. This is normally a common practice with our group if we have any concern that the route may exceed the length of our rope or if it there is any concern of shortage. In this case, I had read information about the area and this route in particular looking for information prior to heading out. The information provided from other climbers never stated that a 70m rope would not be long enough for the route. It's a popular, 3½ star route, so I would have thought if there were any descending issues that they would be noted. Having said that, the length of the route should have given me the information I needed. The route itself is 130 feet long, thus requiring 260 feet of rope. My 70m only measures 230 feet. Even with rope stretch, it still isn't long enough. Unfortunately, I didn't pay attention to route length before heading out. From now on, knots will always be placed in rope ends and route length will always be on the top of my mind. (Source: Edited from a report by Chad Mauer, Castle Rock, CO)

FALL OR SLIP ON ICE, INADEQUATE PROTECTION – RUNNING ROPE THREADED THROUGH WEBBING, WEBBING FAILED
Colorado, Vail, Rigid Designator

Late on the morning of March 21, Christopher Boratenski (31) an experienced climber, was climbing the Rigid Designator (WI5) a single pitch, 115-foot ice climb with two companions when he fell.

His climbing partners Oscar and Charlotte Fors had climbed the route the day before and used an existing tree-anchor at the top of the climb. After leading the climb, Oscar backed up the existing anchor, a steel carabiner in red 1/2-inch webbing backed up by a sling of black 1/2-inch webbing, with a 5mm spectra cord. Oscar rappelled down on double rope and Charlotte followed the climb on top-rope using the steel carabiner with the two back ups as anchor.

On the day of the accident, Chris led the route and used the existing anchor at the top of the climb, but failed to include the steel carabiner, leaving the rope threaded through the black 1/2-inch sling and the 5mm spectra cord. He rappelled off on a double rope (2 x 60m, 9.8mm ropes). Charlotte climbed using one of the ropes as top-rope. After approximately 80 feet of climbing, the angle decreases leading up an additional 20 feet to the anchor. Charlotte stopped climbing at this point and was lowered to the ground. Oscar tied in and climbed to the same point where Charlotte stopped and was lowered to the ground. Chris tied in and climbed again. As Charlotte belayed, she noticed a slight "stickiness" in the rope, but considering ~150 feet of rope is out and the rope seemed to be moving well, she continued to take.

Choosing the partly overhanging right side of the fall, Chris hung on the rope to rest twice on his ascent. He toped out at the same height as the previous climbers and was lowered a few feet before the anchor failed, causing him to fall straight to the ground not touching the icefall on the descent. He landed flat on his back approximately 20 feet below the belay stance, then bounced off the ice pyramid at the base of the ice-fall coming to rest an additional 15 feet farther down. He regained consciousness after about 30 seconds and had severe difficulty breathing. With the help of two other climbers, Chris' position on the slope was secured to the backboard (from rescue cache on site). On advice from the 911 operator, we agreed not to move Chris down the slope to the road (ten minutes steep downhill walk) until additional help arrived. The first paramedics arrived 30 minutes after the 911 call, with additional rescuers arriving over the next hour. The Vail Fire Department, Eagle County Ambulance District, and Vail Mountain Rescue Group personnel, used two 600-foot ropes to lower Boratenski down the steep slope. He was then pulled by snowmobile and transported to a waiting ambulance, which brought him to the Vail Valley Medical Center. Chris was checked into the ER in Vail three hours after his fall. He sustained critical injuries, including broken ribs and nose, punctured lung and nine crushed/broken vertebras.

Analysis

The accident could have been avoided by using the existing steel carabiner in the anchor system. While the anchor would have been adequate for rappelling on double rope, webbing should never be used for a running rope. The repeated climbing and lowering sawed through the black sling and the 5mm spectra cord failed to back up the already running rope. The cut surfaces on both the sling and the cord were burned.

All three climbers were skilled and experienced ice climbers. Chris knew how to set top rope anchors, but considered only the double rope rappel when setting up his initial rappel after leading the climb and did not consider that it may be used as a top rope anchor. The other climbers might have asked for specifics about how the anchor was threaded when Chris came down from his initial rappel, or if either of the two other climbers had checked the anchor when they reached the top of the climb on their respective climbs, then the accident would likely not have occurred.

This fall would likely have had a fatal outcome had it not been thanks to the proximity to the road and Vail's excellent care facilities. Thanks to the Vail Fire department, Mountain Rescue, Vail Valley Medical Center and the supporting climbers for making the evacuation successful. (Source: Oscar Fors, mountainproject.com)

FALL OR SLIP ON ROCK, ROCK FLAKE CAME OFF, PLACED INADEQUATE PROTECTION

Colorado, Eldorado Canyon State Park, West Ridge

On April 13, my climbing partner Dave and I (Scott Bennett, 23) were psyched to be out in Eldo. Our destination was the West Ridge-Sidewall area, my favorite cragging hangout in the canyon. After warming up on Court Jester, I felt ready to get back on my goal: the Unbroken Chain

(5.11c)-False Prophet (5.11d) link-up. I had tried it once about a month back, and was lucky enough to on-sight the first half before falling on the False Prophet crux.

The crux of the pitch is up high, and I got caught looking ahead. I fell about 20-25 feet up when my foot unexpectedly slipped. I felt the normal acceleration and then the comforting deceleration of the rope coming taught. Then the feeling I had been fearing: the sudden "pop" of the flake blowing, the flake that contained my only gear. I landed on the thankfully flat, but painfully solid rock. I hit on my back and immediately I knew I was hurt. I tried to remain still while spewing a string of curses, which probably didn't reassure Dave. Having luckily avoided hitting my head in the fall (yes, I had a helmet), I was quickly able to inventory the damage: scraped elbows, bruised heel, a tweaked wrist, and a disturbingly painful back. After lying down for a while and [engaging in some] nervous discussion, I decided to test out my back and sit up. Painful, but not devastating.

About an hour later, feeling better now, and relieved at the arrival of my friends Matt and Zach, we started down the hill. It took a while, but we made it, including the crux river crossing at the end. A trip to the clinic for some x-rays revealed no broken bones, despite a really painful wrist and nagging back pain.

Analysis

Climbing is dangerous and falling on dangerous routes has consequences. Unbroken Chain is probably harder now, since that flake was a really great hold. I guess it was always a dangerous route, but now more obviously so. The biggest lesson I'm taking from this experience is to place gear! There's no good gear on that part of the route, but there were some small RP placements that I skipped. There's also a cam placement in the sidewall corner (on a giant sling) that I used on my first attempt, although that probably wouldn't have helped. Regardless, taking the time to work that extra piece of gear may prevent dire consequences in the future. (Source: Scott Bennett from a posting on mountainproject.com)

FALL ON SNOW, UNABLE TO SELF-ARREST, CLIMBING ALONE
Colorado, Rocky Mountain National Park, Flattop Mountain

On May 11 between 1100 and 1200, a man (57) fell approximately 50-100 feet while climbing a 45-degree snow colouir on the northwest flank of Flattop Mountain and was unable to self-arrest. An island of rocks in the couloir stopped his fall. His impact with these rocks resulted in serious injuries, including a broken pevlis. He managed to down-climb 1000 feet to the base of the couloir that was still more than five miles away from the trailhead. By the time a pair of backcountry skiers found him on the following day, the injured climber had become hypothermic and disoriented. The skiers reported the accident to the NPS at 1200. An NPS team responded by 1530. They packaged the climber into a litter and evacuated him.

Analysis

This climber had the odds stacked against him in several ways: as the snow warmed up it would have been more likely to "ball-up" on his crampons; inconsistant snow surfaces in the couloir during his climb would have made kicking good steps and finding good footing more difficult; recently exposed rocks would have been more likely to melt out and fall; and self arrest near the top of the couloir was not likely to work if he did fall. The climber stated that he could not remember what had caused his fall, but any of the previously mentioned things could have contributed to it.

The urge to continue with one's plan frequently overshadows continuous reassessment of conditions and the ability to deal with them. On many occasions the conditions do not cooperate with climber's planned objectives. A willingness to remain flexible and to change one's plan as conditions change often results in safer more enjoyable outings.

This climber also elected to climb by himself. Solo climbing always magnifies the risks associated with climbing. In addition, he did not leave a plan with anyone nor did he have a reliable means of communicating with the outside world.

He owes his life to the two skiers who happened to find him and intiate his rescue. (Source: Edited from a report by Mark Pita, Search & Rescue Program Manager, Rocky Mountain National Park)

FALL ON ROCK, CLIMBING UNROPED
Colorado, Boulder Canyon, Avalon Crag

On the morning of Monday June 15, a 17-year-old male was climbing with five others when he decided to free-solo the lower part of the Avalon climbing area, located on the South side of Boulder Creek. This area hosts a number of moderate climbs 5.8 to 5.10 sport routes and is popular on weekends.

The teen climbed approximately 40 feet when another member of the group advised him to stop and they would get him a rope to assist him in descending. Witnesses explained that he slipped, fell, and tumbled several times before landing against a log at the base of the cliff. He suffered a laceration to his head, shoulder area and pain to his ankle. Rocky Mountain Rescue Group set up a "Tyrolean" to move the patient across the creek. The patient was transported to Boulder Community Hospital. (Source: Press Release from Boulder County Sheriff's Office Emergency Services Coordinator)

FALL ON SNOW
Colorado, Capitol Peak, Northwest Ridge

On Friday July 10, James Flowers (47), an experienced climber from

Colorado Springs, and his partner set out to climb the Northwest Ridge of Capitol Peak (14,130 feet), one of the most challenging fourteeners in Colorado. They successfully reached the summit and were descending along the Northwest Ridge when Flowers lost his footing on a snow/ice patch between K2 and Daly Saddle. He fell and slid at high speed through snow chutes and rock bands until he came to rest at an elevation of 12,500 feet in a rocky area.

Flowers initially survived the fall. His climbing partner called his own wife at 2:45 p.m. Friday and she contacted authorities in Aspen. The Pitkin County Sheriff's Office mobilized Mountain Rescue Aspen and a Flight for Life helicopter, the first of which had mechanical problems and was unable to depart from Frisco. Authorities were able to maintain periodic cellphone contact with the climbing partner.

A Denver-based helicopter was sent and due to the altitude, did an initial fly-over before offloading some weight and dropping off a paramedic. The chopper then picked up Mountain Rescue Aspen strike-team members one at a time and dropped them off on a knoll about a mile and a half from Flowers. A Mountain Rescue Aspen paramedic didn't reach Flowers until 6:25 p.m. When the paramedic arrived, Flowers didn't have a pulse and was not breathing. The paramedic performed CPR, which was unsuccessful.

Flowers reportedly had significant injuries to his head, legs and back. He was pronounced dead at the scene. His friend was flown out Friday evening. The three-person team spent the night near the body. A helicopter removed Flowers' body from the mountain Saturday morning. (Source: From an article by Troy Hooper, *Aspen Daily News*, July 12, 2009)

Analysis

The same reporter said, "Most climbing accidents occur during descent." In actuality, most accidents occur ascending in the U.S. (See Table III.) The exact cause of this fall is not known, but we do know that over the years, Capital Peak has seen many similar scenarios. (Source: Jed Williamson)

OFF ROUTE, FALL ON ROCK
Colorado, Rocky Mountain National Park, Lumpy Ridge

My partner and I (ages not recorded) were climbing White Whale (5.7) at Lumpy Ridge on July 15. It is considered by many as a fantastic three-pitch trad route. Neither of us had done the route before. My partner began leading the third and final pitch, then got off route, apparently following a 5.8 R/X crack. She was able to get herself to a small ledge then continued climbing a crack up the face.

Moments later she yelled, "Watch me!" a couple of times, then fell. When she fell the rope went very slack. During her fall, she caught her foot on the ledge and fell below it. I was able to arrest her fall about three feet below the ledge. Her last piece caught her fall. She was able to get back on the climb following the ledge to the tree for the regular belay. Striking the ledge injured her foot, but she had no idea how bad it was. She was able to hike out with the assistance of a walking stick, but still insisted on carrying her pack. She drove herself to Boulder and stopped at the hospital, where she was diagnosed with a Lisfranc fracture. The Lisfranc fracture is a fracture and dislocation of the joints in the mid-foot, where a cluster of small bones forms an arch on top of the foot between the ankle and the toes. From this cluster the metatarsals, extend to the toes. She broke the two middle meta-tarsals and she lost the Lisfranc tendon, which required surgery to reattach.

Analysis

Always plan ahead. A route map or route description is a good resource to have, especially if one is unfamiliar with the route. Down-climbing is an essential skill all climbers should possess. (Source: From a post on rock-climbing.com, July 29, 2009)

ROCKFALL, FALL ON ROCK
Colorado, Boulder Canyon, Redgarden Wall

I was on pitch 4 of Rewritten (5.7) on August 1 when the party above me yelled down that the block was loose. I've climbed Rewritten before and I knew about the infamous refrigerator block balanced on the ledge above me. I didn't think too much about the warning and kept climbing. When I got to the block, I carefully traversed around it, but when I came to the right side of the block, I stepped on a rock and my foot sank, nudging the block just enough causing it to move. I thought it might miss me, but then it hit my rope and forced me off the ledge headfirst. I ended up falling the entire pitch and was about even with my belayer when the rope finally stopped me! I yelled, "Rock!" as loud as I could, but "rock" was an understatement! I knew others were directly below me and was VERY relieved to find that they were ok. The route was completely covered in dust, pebbles, and some good-sized pieces of rock. After walking around the base of the cliff, I found tree limbs and exploded rock everywhere. My partner's pack was destroyed along with some of its contents. I am thankful that nobody got seriously hurt and that I was wearing my helmet.

Analysis

Loose rock is a common occurrence in many climbing areas. The best way to manage this objective hazard is to, if possible, avoid climbing in areas where loose rock is a known hazard; don't climb below other parties; don't stage, or socialize at the base of suspect routes; evaluate rock integrity as you climb; test holds before committing to them; tread lightly around loose rock; and, of course, wear a helmet. (Source: Micah Issac, Boulder, CO, from a report on mountainproject.com)

FALL ON ROCK, INADEQUATE BELAY – ROPE RAN THROUGH DEVICE AND NO KNOT IN ROPE ENDS
Colorado, Boulder Canyon, Bihedral Wall

On August 19, 2009 Andrea Knufken (29) and her partner were climbing on a route, possibly Trick or Treat (5.8) - a single-pitch climb on the upper tier of the Bihedral Wall. A climber who witnessed the fall heard Andrea, saw her bounce off the belay ledge and fall down a rock gully until by-standing climbers jumped on her rope and arrested the fall. She was lowered to the ground and received care until Rocky Mountain Rescue Group arrived. Apparently her belayer had not tied into or tied a knot into the end of the rope. After Andrea led the climb and was being lowered, the rope-end ran through the belay device causing the fall. Andrea fell between 10 and 30 feet and hit several ledges, sustaining injuries to her face, head and right knee.

Analysis

The routes in this section are all bolted and approximately 100 feet in length with a weird slabby section for the bottom ten feet of the climb. A fifty-meter rope or a short sixty-meter rope may not be long enough to lower the leader all the way to the base of the climb. Closing the belay system by placing a knot on the end of the rope, anchoring the rope, or have the belayer tie into the rope could have prevented the rope from being pulled through the belay device. (Source: Britton Calvert, Boulder, CO)

FALL ON ROCK, INADEQUATE PROTECTION and TOO MUCH TIME TO PLACE PROTECTION
Colorado, Lovers Leap

On September 6, Greg (40s), Mike (30s) and I, Matt (50), were planning to do Lover's Leap (5.7), switching leads and having the two following climbers simul-climb as seconds on separate ropes. I took the first lead, with the intention of linking Pitch 1 and Pitch 2 to make the leads more interesting on the remainder of the climb. I bypassed the first belay ledge, placing a runner on one of the bolts for protection, and proceeded to climb out on the 5.8 wall that was slightly off route. At this point I had used approximately 37 meters (120 feet) of rope. Realizing that the wall offered little in the way of protection, I moved into a dihedral above the ledge. I was approximately 15 feet above the ledge at this point with what I thought were two good feet and one good hand. I identified a crack in which to place a cam above my head, but as I reached down with my left hand, I felt myself coming off the rock and shouted, "Take!" which Mike did. I hit the belay ledge before extending what could have been a 24 to 30-foot whipper, but in light of the 5.7+ nature of the climb, I might also have hit some other feature before the rope caught.

Upon hitting the ledge I felt no pain, did a self-assessment, and determined that I was physically ok but for an odd looking right ankle. Within a few seconds, my right ankle opened with an 8-inch long, 4-inch laceration that I assumed to be a compound fracture. I shouted down to my climbing partners that I had a compound fracture and that they should call 911. I then tied myself off to the bolt on the ledge and used a bandana and first aid materials to wrap my bleeding right ankle. Greg, belayed by Mike, climbed to my aid and rendered additional first aid. Michael remained below on the phone with rescue personnel and directed the Alpine Search and Rescue (ASAR) team out of Evergreen Colorado to the ledge when they arrived.

ASAR sent up a climber and a medic. The climber rigged a top-roped rappel and the medic rendered additional first aid and did further assessment of my injury. I descended on a tandem rappel with the medic. Upon standing up to rappel, the pain hit me in earnest. I was evacuated to an ambulance over steep and difficult terrain by the outstanding, hardworking, and heroic volunteers of ASAR.

I ended up with a fractured heel. The laceration was unrelated to the fracture and appears to have resulted from my climbing shoe rubber sticking hard on the ledge as my foot continued to move. End result of the injury is an internal fixation of the comminuted fracture of the heel with eight screws and a titanium plate, a full month in the hospital, and months of rehab yet to come.

Analysis

Always get protection in quickly when climbing above a ledge, especially when trying to make a relatively easy climb more interesting! (Source: Matthew Y. Biscan, Denver, CO)

FALL ON ROCK, PLACED INADEQUATE PROTECTION, PROTECTION PULLED OUT, EXCEEDING ABILITIES
Colorado, Clear Creek Canyon

Sept. 13th. It was a beautiful day for climbing. Michelle (24) and I (29) drove out to Clear Creek Canyon to hone our fledgling lead skills. We were both cautious, yet eager climbers with moderate skill. decided to climb Mounty, a 5.7 trad route. The beta we had gotten from mountainproject.com had indicated that the pro was small but solid. Although I wasn't a very experienced trad leader (I had only lead trad 8 or 9 times before this route), I was a confident 5.7 climber, so I wasn't very worried about the small pro. We were on a ledge, so I built a belay anchor for Michelle before starting up. After 25 feet of climbing, I had only found placements for three small pieces: two nuts and a #1 (blue) mastercam. I clipped the rope through the carabiner attached directly to the mastercam's integrated sling. At this point, I found that I had gotten a bit off-route and traversed a bit up and to the left to get back on to the main crack. When I reached the main crack, I was not feeling very good about the amount of pro I had in and I was anxious to get in another piece before climbing higher. I had difficulty finding a placement. I wasn't comfortable continuing the climb without more pro, so I decided to down-climb. It turns out that being a confident 5.7 climber doesn't translate into being a confident 5.7 down-climber. While I was traversing down and to the right, back towards the blue cam, I slipped. The cam pulled out, and the two nuts were too low to catch me, so I hit the ground. I sustained an ulna fracture at the elbow and a fifth metacarpal fracture, but I was otherwise fine. Michelle made a sling for my arm, we hiked out, and she drove me to the hospital.

Analysis

Several mistakes were made that led to this accident. The biggest mistake was leading a route that was not well protected as a beginning trad leader. I knew from my research online that the route was not easily protected, but I decided to climb it anyway. My second mistake was that I didn't turn around earlier when I had trouble in the beginning finding placements. My third mistake was clipping the cam's integrated sling before changing the direction of the climb, instead of clipping a runner. It's possible that rope-drag could have caused the cam to walk and the placement to worsen. My fourth and fifth mistakes were overestimating my down-climbing abilities and not practicing down-climbing frequently enough while top-roping. (Source: Sent in with no last name)

INADEQUATE BELAY, CLIMBER LOWERED OFF END OF ROPE, INADEQUATE EQUIPMENT — ROPE TOO SHORT
Colorado, Clear Creek Canyon, Highlander Crag

On December 20, 2009, a 35-year-old man climbing with his girlfriend fell 20 to 25 feet. They were climbing in Clear Creek Canyon on Herb-a-Veg-A-Matic. Joe Pierzchala, climbing on a nearby route, witnessed the fall and gives this account:

The climber was being lowered after having led the route, draws still in place. Suddenly he was free falling! After lowering my partner, we observed the climber tied into his end of the rope, but that the belayer's end was now 35-40 feet up the route. We concluded that the climber was lowered off the end of the rope. We checked the guidebook, which indicated that the route was 102 feet in height, and concluded that the party must have been using a 50m rope. The fall distance corresponds to the distance a 50m rope would have come up short. The fallen climber landed on his back, narrowly missing a very large rock that could have caused more serious injuries. It appeared that the climber did land on a smaller rock, however, which likely caused injury to his back/pelvis/hip.

Analysis

Climbers are encouraged to: 1) read the guidebook re: the length of the route; 2) know the length of one's rope; 3) make sure one's equipment (rope, protection, etc.) is sufficient to climb the chosen route; 4) tie a stopper knot in the belayer's end of the rope, tying into the rope or tying off the end of the rope; and 5) ensure better communication between partners. Two other important ingredients are research and experience.

Clear Creek Canyon is well known as a predominantly sport climbing area developed for use with 60m ropes and is also well known for having a number of routes that require a 70m rope. Using a 50m rope in Clear Creek Canyon is a major oversight on equipment selection. (Source: Joe Pierzchala, Denver, CO)

(Editor's Note: There was one fatality in the Boulder Falls area in September but there are not enough details to provide a full narrative. What we know is that a man (40) fell while being belayed on the route Empor. Neither the climber nor belayer was wearing helmets. We think this might be yet another case in which the belay rope is not long enough and it goes through the belay device.

Another fatality was reported by Tim Kline on Mountain Project web site. Kline and his partner were climbing Lovers Leap when they spotted a body at the bottom of the cliff. The unidentified free-solo climber had been dead for a day or two. No further information was available, but the key ingredients—climbing alone and unroped—warrant reporting here.)

FOOTHOLD BROKE OFF – FALL ON ROCK
Idaho, City of Rocks National Reserve, Castle Rock

On May 21 at 11:45 a.m., volunteer camp host Dottie Cross (63) broke a foothold and fell while attempting to lead the upper pitch of "One For Matt" on Castle Rock. Her climbing companion, Duane Ackerman (62)of Elba, Idaho, lowered Cross to his belay point at the 100-foot level. She was convinced that her right lower leg was broken.

Ackerman rappelled to the ground and utilized Cross's park radio to call for help. The climbing ranger and two-trail crew responded from nearby Bracksiecks Pillar trail and base called 911 to request an ambulance at 12:15. Five additional park staff responded to help.

Upon arrival at the scene, the climbing ranger ascended the first pitch with a Mini Traxion Pulley self-belay on Ackerman's line, trailing an 11mm low stretch rescue rope. Dottie Cross was found hanging in her harness from the anchor chains. She was alert, oriented, smiling. She stated her right lower leg was broken but not in excessive pain. She denied any other injury and adamantly refused helicopter transport.

A vacuum splint was applied. The ranger the tandem rappelled with the patient to the ground, with a fireman's belay from below. She was placed in stokes litter and carried out of the approach gully, which is steep and bouldery. Having seven staff and four volunteers in this section was key in order to be able to pass the litter down without too much difficulty.

The rescue team arrived at the Stines Creek Picnic Area and the waiting Life Run ambulance at 1:45 p.m. Throughout, Cross remained alert and oriented and in good spirits.

Cross was transported to Cassia Regional Medical center in Burley, Idaho, where she was diagnosed with complete and comminuted fractures of her right tibia and fibula, just below knee level. She underwent successful surgery on the evening of the 21st.

Analysis

Thanks to an alert belay and her proximity to the last bolt, Dottie only fell about ten or fifteen feet. However, the second pitch of the route "One For Matt" is 5.8 on less than vertical, very featured rock, which is typical of routes on Castle Rock. Falling on this terrain is like falling with crampons on. Your feet will catch and a lower leg injury will result. Often times in a longer fall, the climber will have a combination of a lower leg injury and an injury to the back of the head as they fall past the tripping point. This illustrates that moderate to easy ground can be more dangerous than harder, steeper terrain.

"One For Matt" was at the time a brand-spanking new route. Dottie and Duane were making the third ascent. There is a fair chance that the foothold that broke had never been stood upon or never weighted so hard. (Source: Brad Schilling, Climbing Ranger, City of Rocks National Reserve)

FALL ON ROCK, INADEQUATE BELAY — ROPE TOO SKINNY FOR BELAY DEVICE (GRIGRI)
Kentucky, Red River Gorge, Torrent Falls

On April 11, Marie Abernathey (early 20s) was leading Dream of a Bee (5.8), a well-bolted sport climb at the Torrent Falls area of Red River Gorge. Abernathey was being belayed by Katherine West (early 20s), a new climber who was using a Petzl Grigri. Above the last bolt and below the anchors, Abernathey fell. West, in an attempt to arrest the fall, squeezed the rope tightly with her non-brake hand (which was on the rope above the belay device). The device failed to lock, which caused Abernathey to fall 60 feet to the ground at near-freefall speed. Just above the ground, Abernathey impacted a three-foot-high boulder, injuring her back. She was stabilized and a climber with medical training treated her with pain medication. After about 30 minutes, the climbers in her party helped Abernathey walk to a cabin about 100 yards down the trail from the crag. West sustained burns to her left hand from attempting to halt the 60-foot fall. Neither required a hospital visit, and both were able to enjoy the Red River Gorge Reunion festivities that night.

Analysis

After the accident, several climbers from other parties verified that the device was rigged properly and passed several "auto-lock tug tests." The device itself was fully functional.

Petzl's user manual for the Grigri states the device is designed for a 10mm to 11mm rope. In this case, the climbers where using a 9.4mm cord. The owner of the rope had used the same rope and belay device numerous times before without incident. Similarly, many climbers either disregard or are unaware of Petzl's rope diameter recommendation and still manage to climb safely due to proper belay technique, since a Grigri will lock and hold a fall provided that the belayer keeps his or her brake hand in the correct position to arrest the fall.

A proper belay would have prevented this accident, even though the party was using a rope that is skinnier than what is recommended by Petzl. It is important to use proper belay technique, even with an auto-locking belay device. Also, if someone is learning to belay, it is a good idea to have an experienced climber hold the rope below the new belayer's brake hand. In the event of the belay getting away from the new belayer, the other climber can lock off the rope.

Additionally, using a rope that is within the manufacturers specifications for the belay device may have prevented this accident. The belay device is designed to lock automatically. However, it is possible that even with a thicker rope, the belayer's hand squeezing the rope above the device may have relieved just enough force from the Grigri cam that the device did not lock automatically.

Bottom line: either a proper belay, a backup/safety observer for the new belayer, or using the correct rope for the belay device would have prevented this accident. (Source: Lucas Gruenther)

AVALANCHE, POSSIBLE POOR POSITION CHOICE
Montana, Gallatin Range, Hyalite Canyon

On Thursday morning, December 10th, at 0700 a group of 24 (12 teams) participants lined up in the Grotto Falls parking lot for the 4th annual Ice Breaker ice climbing competition. Each team climbs as many difficult routes as possible in a day. Around 0845, competitors Guy Lacelle (54) and his partner Adam Knoff completed the ice climb The Dribbles and traversed into the gully leading up to The Climb, above The Dribbles. During this time, two other competitors were climbing The Dribbles with the same objective, although they approached it after climbing a separate set of nearby routes. At 0900, one of them triggered a small avalanche (six inches deep) that caught both him and his partner, carrying them approximately 300 feet down the gully and over a 25-foot ice step where they stopped. One of them ended up going over this precipice headfirst while the other cascaded over the cliff on his back. Both climbers were shaken up but unharmed. They continued back up the gully.

Guy Lacelle and Adam Knoff moved into the gully that the other two were ascending after the first slide. They had no idea anyone was below them, while Lacelle and Knoff thought the party above was already on the ice much higher. Knowing the avalanche danger, the other two hugged the edges of the gully on rocks as much as possible. One wrote in an email, "We assessed the gully above and decided we could continue up and stay out of harm's way. We had not, however, considered that someone might be below us. We were already up there so we might as well go for it, we thought. We decided to at least have a look at the gully above the last crown.

"Continuing up, we skirted the right side of the gully staying mostly on the rocks. We heard no collapsing and saw no cracking, thus deciding to continue up." They reached a point where the gully narrowed and forced them away from the edge. This tapering of the gully forced him to step towards the center where he triggered the second slide.

This second avalanche broke 40 feet across and 18 inches deep on a firm bed surface. The two competitors were able to avoid being caught, but the slide picked up momentum as it moved down the gully towards Lacelle and Knoff. One of the climbers above yelled, "Avalanche!" as he looked down and saw Knoff cresting the second ice bulge.

"Worse than the sound of collapsing snow was the sound of someone below us, who turned out to be Knoff yelling to Lacelle." Unfortunately, Lacelle was in the middle of the second ice step and was unable to avoid the avalanche. He was swept about 1,000 vertical feet to his death, the last 400 feet being the steep ice cliff of Silken Falls.

Knoff descended the gully and rappelled the falls in search of Lacelle. Before descending, Knoff directed the climbers above to probe the debris uphill of the falls to confirm that Lacelle was swept over the edge. Halfway down the rappel Knoff saw Lacelle's boot sticking out of the snow at the bottom of the climb. He alerted the others of his discovery. He continued down and found Lacelle with his head down hill and fully buried except for one boot sticking out of the snow. Knoff dug him out but was unable to revive him. The other two climbers rappelled down and were on the scene within minutes. Knoff left them with the body and he descended to alert SAR about the accident.

Analysis

We investigated the avalanche on Friday, December 11th. The avalanche that struck the victim consisted of pencil-hard wind slab, 46-cm thick, sitting on 5-20 cm of weak facets. Hyalite experienced cold temperatures, strong winds and light precipitation over a four-day span before the event.

The steep, narrow gullies of Hyalite Canyon were loaded with wind-blown snow and from snow cascading down its steep faces. On Thursday, December 10th, numerous human triggered avalanches were reported in Hyalite over the course of the day, most of them small pockets of wind slab triggered by other Ice Breaker climbers crossing slopes.

The advisory on December 10th read, "Today, the primary concerns are wind slabs formed by recent west and northwest winds. While these wind slabs do not appear very sensitive they are widespread and human triggered avalanches are possible. For this reason the avalanche danger is rated MODERATE."

The only thoughts on the analysis have to do with the human factor. The amount of its influence in this accident are unknown, but certainly worth considering. The main one is the fact that this was an ice climbing competition. This complicated things because it was an over-riding factor in decision-making. Would the climbers above Guy Lacelle and Adam Knoff have kept climbing after they got caught in the first avalanche had it not been a competition? Would Guy and Adam have climbed underneath another party headed toward their intended route if it was just a routine day of climbing? These are unanswerable, but for climbers in this situation in the future, certainly worth thinking about. (Source: Eric Knoff, Doug Chabot, and Mark Staples, Avalanche Specialists)

FALL ON ICE, NO EXPERIENCE
New Hampshire, Cathedral Ledge

In February, two inexperienced climbers in their early 20s (never climbed ice before) signed out boots, crampons, and ice tools from the demo people at the annual IMCS Mount Washington Valley Ice Festival. They bought some used ice screws and headed for Cathedral Ledge. Witnesses stated that they looked shaky at best as the leader headed up the pitch. At the third screw placement, the leader fell, leaving both tools in the ice. The second lowered him to the ground and untied him. With some leg injuries and a cut face, they headed for the hospital. Climbers reported the axes, rope, and screws were left in the ice. The demo people went to Cathedral and retrieved their gear. Boots and crampons were returned after the hospital visit, and we returned the ropes and screws to the climbers. (Source: Rick Wilcox, International Mountain Equipment)

Analysis

We don't even like to count this one as a climbing accident. But it is. One important question for people who are responsible for handing out demo gear of any kind is whether they can/should refuse to lend the gear if they believe the individuals requesting it are not experienced enough. (Source: Jed Williamson)

AVALANCHE, UNABLE TO SELF-ARREST
New Hampshire, Mount Washington, Tuckerman Ravine

On April 11, Daniel Zucker (46) from Danville, VT, and Tim Finnocchio (31), both athletic and experienced mountaineers, were climbing the steep snow route known as "Dodge's Drop" unroped, each with two technical ice axes and crampons. They had recently climbed Hillman's Highway and were familiar with the terrain on the Boott Spur Ridge. The plan was to climb the route to access the hiking trails to the summit of Mount Washington, then descend through Tuckerman Ravine.

For much of the climb, the surface conditions were refrozen springtime crust. The party reported they were enjoying the climbing conditions when on this surface. At times they encountered small areas of newer softer snow, but this surface was more difficult to climb, so they opted for the old surface when possible. Nearing the top of the climb, they encountered an isolated pocket of relatively new slab. Zucker reported he was unable to swing his axes through the new snow into the crust, his boots were getting full penetration when kicked into the snow, and the snow was fully supporting his weight. He stated that he decided to move left to get around the slab, both for stability reasons and for the easier climbing on the crust. As he was working himself toward the edge of the slab, the avalanche released.

Zucker recognized what was transpiring and was able to see the fracture line propagate upwards from his feet to a point about six to eight feet above him. The fracture then propagated outward and the slab began to slide downhill. Finnocchio was about ten feet below and slightly to the side of Zucker. He had both ice tools sunk into the snow. The initial slab, in which Zucker was entrained, pulled out more snow above Finnoccio. He attempted to hold on against the force of the slab pouring over him, but he was eventually pulled off his stance. Both individuals were carried downhill, and each reported being airborne at some point. Zucker stated he was impressed by how much time he had during the course of the slide to figure out what to do. He said he was unsure of whether to try to self-arrest or swim to stay on top. At one point he discarded one tool and attempted to self-arrest with the other. He felt the pick engaging the crust but was unable to stop himself. He also reported that during this time he saw his partner slide past him, indicating he at least managed to slow himself to some degree.

The avalanche carried them over a small cliff (hence Zucker reporting being airborne for "three heartbeats") and down into a treed slope below. The compressive force of the snow impacting the slope below the cliff was quite strong; it ripped both ice axes out of Finnocchio's hands, and they both felt as though their clothes and gear were also being pulled loose. They came to rest in the trees with most of the debris, though some of the debris continued to run farther down-slope. Both individuals came to rest on top of the snow. No excavation was required.

Zucker suffered a small laceration on his forehead, a broken pinky finger, sprained ankle, some ligament damage in his knee, bruising on his thigh and shin, and abrasions on both elbows. The abrasions were caused by sliding on the icy crust while wearing only a synthetic t-shirt. Finnocchio reported that he lost his vision momentarily when they came to rest but regained it soon after. He also suffered multiple abrasions on arms and hands, ligament damage in one knee, and a bruised pelvis. The climbers were escorted to the Snow Ranger cabin at Hermit Lake where they were more thoroughly assessed and treated. From here, they were transported to the parking lot in the USFS Snowcat, where they were released into their own vehicle for transportation to a local hospital.

Analysis

These two climbers were incredibly fortunate. This route is generally considered "no-fall" territory due to numerous rocks, cliffs, and trees in the fall line. The total vertical drop of their fall is estimated to be around 800 feet. They managed to pass through the rocky section of the fall un-scathed, with the injuries being sustained only after being carried into the trees. Ironically the avalanche that caused their fall likely helped protect them from more significant injuries, as they probably rode on the debris cushion to their resting point. Falling this distance with crampons on, ice tools in hand, and going over small cliffs usually concludes much worse. That they were able to walk themselves down from an incident such as this is remarkable, to say the least.

The weather forecast had called for mostly cloudy skies, summit tem-peratures falling to 15 degrees F, and winds ranging from 25-40 mph. The morning avalanche advisory discussed the snowpack staying frozen for most of the day, with the best chance of warm soft snow being on south-facing aspects. Northerly aspects were expected to remain cold and frozen through the day.

From an avalanche perspective, the climbers had chosen a reasonable route. Although Dodge's Drop is not one of the forecasted areas on the mountain, it is adjacent to Hillman's Highway, which is one the eight slopes and gullies of Tuckerman Ravine subject to Avalanche Advisories. All eight areas were forecasted at "Low" at the time of the accident and where heavily skied without incident.

Many valuable lessons can be learned from this event. Two are offered here, as they are not uncommon occurrences on Mount Washington. First, it's important to recognize that "Low avalanche danger" does not mean "No avalanche danger." Isolated pockets of instability can be present under a "Low" rating; recognizing and assessing this hazard rests with the individual. Second, it underscores the importance of being able to assess hazards before dropping in over the top of them. In this instance, there was at least one skier known to be hiking up Hillman's with the intention of descending Dodge's Drop. It's quite likely that this skier would have triggered the pocket if the climbers had not. Whether the hazard is avalanches, crevasses, undermined snow, etc., it's always a good idea to assess for hazards before descending from above.

FALL ON SNOW – UNABLE TO SELF-ARREST
New Hampshire, Tuckerman Ravine, Left gully

On March 14, a woman fell approximately 1,200 feet from near the top of Left Gully in Tuckerman Ravine. She was unable to self-arrest and quickly lost her ice ax, as she rapidly accelerated on the very slick surface. Along the way, her crampon caught the surface, resulting in an open angulated lower leg fracture. She also suffered arm and rib injuries before coming to a stop low in the floor of Tuckerman Ravine. Snow Rangers, MWVSP, and AMC personnel responded, treated her injuries, and packaged her into a litter. The litter was belayed down the Little Headwall to the top of the Sherburne Ski Trail. From there a snowmobile transported the litter to an ambulance waiting at Pinkham Notch Visitor Center.

FALL ON ICE – UNABLE TO SELF-ARREST
New Hampshire, Huntington Ravine, Central Gully

Approximately 15 minutes after being notified of the incident described above, Snow Rangers learned of a second incident unfolding in Huntington Ravine. A mountaineer had fallen from somewhere between the top of the Fan and the ice bulge in Central Gully. He slid approximately 1,000 feet through icy talus before coming to rest near the base of Huntington Ravine. He suffered numerous significant injuries, including a mid-shaft femur fracture. Bystanders began to provide care while assistance was sought out. By the time the Snow Rangers arrived, the victim was conscious and in severe pain. He was splinted and packaged into a litter, which was belayed one rope length to flat ground at the base of the Ravine, due to the icy surface. The USFS snowcat transported the victim to a waiting ambulance at Pinkham Notch Visitor Center.

Analysis

These two incidents have one strong central theme—that sliding falls on icy surfaces are very difficult to stop. In these cases, the crust was formed three days prior to the incidents with a warm, wet day followed by a sharp drop in temperature. Surfaces immediately became incredibly hard and slick and stayed that way through the Saturday. The morning's Avalanche Advisory stated, "The main safety concern today is the potential for long sliding falls due to the hard icy snow conditions... Bring your crampons, ice ax, and mountaineering experience with you today so you can get around in steep terrain and successfully self-arrest if you slip. If you don't have this equipment and the ability to use it you should stick to low angled terrain."

One lesson we can all take home from these incidents is the importance of practicing your skills in all conditions and avoiding steep terrain on days when the difficulty of the conditions exceeds your ability to self-arrest. Many thanks go out to the numerous bystanders and volunteers who helped out on these incidents. (Source for the above three incidents: www.tuckerman. org and Justin Preisendorfer, Snow Ranger/Backcountry & Wilderness Supervisor)

FALL ON ROCK, INADEQUATE BELAY – LOWERING ERROR
New Hampshire, Rumney, Armed and Dangerous
On Today (April 19) on the route Armed and Dangerous, a seasoned climber was lowered off the end of his rope by another seasoned climber. Both climbers had joked regarding the length of the rope/climb prior to starting the route.

The climber fell 12 feet onto his head and upper back, sustaining only a small head injury and some apparent nerve damage to his arms/pelvis. The climber was extricated by 15+ climbers and 10+ rescuers. He never lost consciousness, and it appears that he will recover fully after some rest and relaxation.
Analysis
He was lucky not only to fall from where he did, but how he did and with so many people around.

Let this be a lesson to tie a knot in the end of your rope, or at least look at the end when lowering off a climb, especially one you haven't been on many times. (Source: Edited from a Mountain Project posting by Ladd Raine)

FALL ON ROCK, CLIMBING ALONE
Nevada, Red Rocks, Rainbow Wall – The Original Route
A climber, Josh, fell from the second pitch (140 feet) to the base of the climb. Three climbers were on the route. Two were climbing together, and the victim of the fall was alone climbing by himself. One person was climbing from the 2nd to the 4th pitch. Two were on separate anchors at the 2nd pitch. One of the two climbers at the 2nd pitch was belaying the climber en route to the 4th pitch. Josh was at the second pitch also and was in the process of setting up a z-rig, or some kind of mechanical advantage system, to haul his big-wall bag from the base of the climb when he dropped six carabiners. He decided to rappel a fixed line in order to retrieve the carabiners. He had a pulley attached at the anchors that was attached to his haul bag and to him. At this point, nobody is sure how it happened, or what he was doing, but he detached from the anchor and somehow fell. As he fell,

the haul bag somewhat counter-balanced him and without a doubt saved his life. However, he suffered substantial injuries.

The helicopter was able to perform a one-skid landing near the base. Basically, they place one of the two skids on the rock, balance the helicopter, and can load/unload on the side where the skid is down. In this instance, Search & Rescue were able to backboard him at the base and load him in the helicopter and fly him out.

Further comment: "Hello everyone. I would first like to thank everyone for the support. I am Josh's brother, and this thread was pointed out to me by one of his friends. Josh is doing considerably well given the circumstances. The previous info is quite accurate, so I will just fill you in on his progress. The fall pulverized his sacrum into '"dust"', as the doctors described it, and his thoracic 5-8 and cervical vertebrae were shattered. He was in surgery for about nine hours, and the surgeon fused his T 5-8, supporting them with rods, and made another rod device to reattach his spine to his pelvis. They did not remove any of his sacrum, and it will eventually re-calcify. Those were the extent of his major injuries. He has two deep lacerations, one on his left elbow and another on his right knee, and he has a concussion, but no broken arms, legs, ribs, no heart or lung damage, and no major brain damage. He is incredibly lucky, which should go without saying. He is already breathing on his own and is expected to be moved out of ICU in the next few days. Again, my family and I would like to thank everyone for showing concern and support in this trying time. It is greatly appreciated." Jeff C.

And another: "Hello all: This is Josh. I am recovering steadily. The doctors' prognosis is quite good for my eventual full mobility recovery, and all are impressed at my current progress. I have two months of bed rest ahead, and several months of physical therapy following.

"I do not remember any of the accident and the events of that morning are fuzzy, too, so I can't provide a good technical do/don't analysis of it. I suspect that, like most accidents, it was due to carelessness on my part. I've been climbing for over ten years, so inexperience likely did not play a role. I thought, like most of us, that it 'could not happen to me'.

"Lessons from my fall:
We hear it again and again: Double/triple check your rappel system.

Wear a helmet. Rock fall did not play a role in this accident, yet, based on the current condition of my old Hugh Banner Kevlar Carbon "EL CAP," it saved my life several times over during this accident and also accounts for the fact that I received only a minor concussion.

Solo climbing is more dangerous than climbing with a partner... not necessarily for the belay aspect. Modern solo belay devices work great. Having a second set of eyes to crosscheck my rigging, etc, might have stopped my accident from happening.

Had there not been a party above me, I may not have been rescued at all. Have fun, stay safe." (Source: From postings on Mountain Project, December 3, 4, and 10, 2009)

FALL ON ROCK – RAPPEL ERROR (NO KNOT IN END OF ROPE), DISTRACTION, HASTE, WEATHER, DARKNESS
New Mexico, Los Alamos, White Rock

It must have been a nightmare. Seriously, I don't do that. I know better. Way better. I've been climbing for over 12 years without an accident and just plain know better. Only rookies do that. Apparently not so.

When I awoke in my bed on Friday morning (August 28), I was hoping it was a nightmare, but when I looked down at my left foot wrapped in a bandage and covered with an ice pack and felt the discomfort coursing up my leg, I was painfully aware it wasn't just a nightmare and I had definitely f*****d up. It could have been worse though...when a climber rappels off the end of his rope it's generally a lot worse than a severely sprained ankle (with torn ligaments), a bruised left ass cheek and a scraped left arm. Yes, I had been very lucky.

On Thursday evening I had driven down to Gallows Edge to replace some anchor hardware on four routes there. I had been given some hardware in support of the Anchor Replacement Initiative (ARI) and wanted to replace some of the weird anchor setups there that involved chain links bolted directly onto the bolt stud using washers. It turns out I didn't need to drill but one new hole because the existing stainless steel bolts looked great. So I just replaced the hardware that was attached to the bolts. Also, while down there, my friends Matthias and Lee had been looking to establish a new route that they had top-roped before.

For all of this work I did what I normally do for working on routes--I setup a single line static rope anchored to some huge blocks. My static line is about 60 feet in length and since I planned to only work on the top of climbs and drill some holes for Matthias and Lee, I didn't need a longer rope. I did all my work with using a Grigri on the single static line which allowed me to rappel down and stop to work with the Grigri locking up on the rope, as designed, while working. I replaced three anchors and drilled the holes/installed the bolts for Matthias and Lee without issue and things were going great. Our friend James showed up and had been planning to climb but his partner bailed on account of the weather. It had rained once while we were down there and it was looking threatening again as the evening wore on.

Matthias and Lee climbed their new route and got ready to head out. I wanted to replace the hardware on a route called Planet of the Apes because it also had some non-standard chain-on-bolt action going on. It was getting darker, but I still had plenty of light to replace this one anchor. So I moved my rope over to this route, leaving it tied around the huge boulder it had been tied around all night. This boulder, though, was some distance from the route I was now working on. Matthias and Lee headed out, but James stuck around to walk out with me after I replaced the anchor. The anchor replacement went fine, but just as I was finishing up, I dropped a piece of the old chain I had removed. By now it was getting pretty dark, an ominous looking storm was brewing to the south and I was engaged in conversation with James. I told him I was going to zip down to the base of the route to pick up that chain and that he could take down the rope once I was off rappel. I started rapping down and got down at least two thirds of the route, maybe more, when I noticed a curious and quick sensation—the rope whipped through my Grigri.

I yelled up to James that I had just rapped off the end of the rope but was OK. I think I might have even said I was off rappel, obviously, in an attempt to lighten up the situation.

I felt my knees and ankles and stood up without issue. I took a few steps and noticed my right side was completely fine. My left side, however, was not as good. My left ankle felt broken, my left knee was sore, my left ass cheek was super tender and my left arm was scraped up pretty good. I could still walk, though. So I told James I'd limp back up there to get my pack and asked him to pack up some of my gear into his pack. All the while, James was staying levelheaded, positive and extremely helpful. I took advantage of the shock and limped quickly around and up to the top to gather my stuff.

James coiled up the rope, we loaded up our packs and donned our headlamps, as it was fully dark by now. Thanks to James taking most of the gear, my pack was pretty light and I limped/hopped up the trail. In places where it was steep I could use the rocks on the side as support and in places where it was flatter, James offered up his shoulder for me to lean on. We slowly moved up and near the top I asked James to go up a bit and drop his pack so he could take mine. He graciously did this and we limped to the car with good efficiency. It took probably 30 minutes to get out whereas normally I can hike that in 15.

At the car, I took off my harness and drank some water while James went back to retrieve his pack from the canyon edge. He came back to the car insisting he drive me home, but I was feeling completely aware, and since I have an automatic car, a screwed up left foot wasn't an issue for driving. I insisted he need not drive me home and called Allison to tell her why I was late. I told her James had helped me out and that my plan was to drive straight to the emergency room because I thought I had a broken ankle. She said she'd meet me there.

James has had some medical training in the past and checked my pupils, palpated my upper and lower body to ensure I didn't do any damage to other parts of my body that weren't my chief complaints and reluctantly let me drive myself home. James' help was invaluable.

I arrived at the hospital around 9:00 p.m. and had beat Allison there, so I limped across the parking lot into the ER. It was a short wait and I was visiting with doctor Chadwick in short order. Dr. Chadwick told me a story of breaking his ankle on a volcano hike somewhere where they did not have very good medical care and how it was quite the ordeal. This made me feel better for sure knowing that there is life after an ankle break/sprain. The nurse cleaned out the scrape on my arm and I had x-rays done on my left elbow and left foot. Dr. Chadwick came back with the good news that my ankle was not broken, but that it had likely torn the ligaments, and that obviously I had sprained it big time.

Analysis

I have taught new climbers how to climb/rappel and stress the importance of tying a simple knot in the end of the rope so something like this doesn't happen, yet I failed to practice what I preach but thankfully got off very lucky. This accident was a result of rushing to get out coupled with being distracted by external forces (and not tying a knot in the end of the rope). If anything, it should serve as an example to others to slow down and pay attention to details even when circumstances are pressing and distracting. (Source From a posting by Jason Halladay on Mountain Project)

(Editor's Note: The best reports—and analyses—come in the first-person. Web sites like Mountain Project are full of these.)

FALL ON ROCK, INADEQUATE PROTECTION, INADEQUATE EQUIPMENT
New Mexico, Sandia Mountains, Gemstone Area

Three friends went out climbing at the Gemstone Area on the climb Seamingly Hard, a run-out 5.10, mixed bolted and natural gear seem that is to the climber's left of Gemstone—one of the Sandia Mountains most popular 5.8 routes. They set out later in the afternoon, but specifically to this area since the slab is north facing and located in the shade. The approach follows a narrow, rocky and vegetated trail with cactus, oaks, and yucca for a total of two miles. The trail breaks out of the bottom of Lower La Cueva Canyon where a major landslide occurred in 1999 and meanders up steeper slopes for 600 feet to gain the Gemstone Slabs climbing area.

The leader (45) climbed up and clipped the first bolt about 15 feet off the sloping belay ledge then continued on. The second bolt is notoriously far from the first, and as the climber gets closer to it, the risk of a ground fall becomes very high. The difficulty of climbing is sustained and the clipping stance a bit precarious. The leader slipped before getting to the second bolt. He fell about 35 feet and hit the deck. He landed on his right leg and suffered a fracture of the foot and ankle dislocation, rendering him unable to hike out. Also, he was not wearing a helmet, resulting in a mild head laceration. His friends were able to call for help via cellphone.

Three Mountain Rescue teams, two fire departments, and the State Police were activated. A Strike Team made its way to the patient and secured him on the ledge and treated his injuries. He was placed into a titanium litter and transported across an exposed traverse to another staging area where a 600-foot guiding line was rigged. The guiding line was instrumental, as it took hours before teams were actually fielded to help out as there were three other Search and Rescue missions happening in the Sandia Mountains and one more in the Jemez Mountains, all at the same time.

Analysis

The climber had 19 years of climbing experience. Although he had not been climbing recently, he was confident but perhaps under-prepared mentally and/or physically and did not have small gear appropriate for protection. No guide book gives credence to the fact that this route is run-out or that ground falls have resulted with similar and worse injuries have happened in the past. This did not help his decision to do this climb. There is no danger rating for this climb (i.e., "R"—meaning run-out, or "X"—meaning that if you fall you can be seriously injured or killed). Most modern bolted routes are protected so that the bolts keep climbers from hitting ledges, the ground, or other objective hazards. This route was put up in 1979 when the ethic was a bit different than it is today in terms of sport climbing crags that mimic indoor climbing.

Doing some research on your climb is an important part of assessing the risk. Risk can be mitigated in part by assessing probability and multiplying it by consequence. (Source: Marc Beverly, President of Strike Rescue and volunteer with the Albuquerque Mountain Rescue Team)

FALLS ON ROCK (12), PROTECTION PULLED OUT (4), DISLOCATIONS (4), INADEQUATE PROTECTION (3), INADEQUATE BELAY, RAPPEL ER-ROR, FALLING OBJECT, OFF ROUTE, EXCEEDING ABILITY, STRAINED GROIN

New York, Mohonk Preserve, Shawangunks

Eighteen reports were submitted for 2009, of which ten occurred in September and October.

The length of the incidents involving falls was from 15-30 feet, though there was one 60-footer that happened as a result of a belay failure. In that case, the climber was caught on a slinged horn and there was no injury.

The average age of the climbers was 40 and the level of route difficulty averaged 5.6. The injuries included five fractures, five sprains/strains, four lacerations, and four dislocations. The latter included one woman (27) who dislocated her knee while putting on her climbing shoes at a rappel station. (This was not counted as an incident.) The other three dislocations (ages 27, 37, and 49) resulted in the climbers having to be lowered. One man (71) with 25 years of experience strained a groin muscle or tendon and had to be lowered.

A man (20) with eight years of experience, according to the report, rappelled off one end of his rope—as his doubled rope was not even. This resulted in a fracture of two of his lumbar vertebrae—but no neurological damage. (Source: From reports submitted by Mohonk Preserve)

FALLING ICE
Oregon, Mount Hood, Southside

On January 21, while ascending the Southside route on Mount Hood at 10,000 feet, a large piece of falling ice hit Brooke Colvin (31) in the face, causing her to fall about 400 feet. Her climbing partner (and husband) descended to her, realized that she was deceased, and continued down to report the accident. A separate party witnessed it and notified authorities by cellphone. A rescue team from Portland Mountain Rescue lowered the body to an awaiting snowcat at the upper Palmer snowfield.

Analysis

The unstable ice near the summit was caused by an unusual early season temperature inversion. The summit ice (heavy rime-ice) becomes a greater risk when warmer temperatures melt the bond holding the rime in place. This is normally due to direct solar heating (greater later in the day and later in the season), but can also result from prolonged elevated air temperatures.

The unstable snow/ice conditions near the summit described above contributed to a large number of accidents on Mount Hood this year. Five climbers were injured in separate accidents caused by falling snow/ice this season. (Source: Jeff Sheetz, Portland Mountain Rescue)

FALL ON SNOW, CLIMBING UNROPED
Oregon, Mount Hood, Southside

On May 17, John Creager (54) was descending a Southside variation on Mount Hood with his two partners. He lost his footing and fell about 400 feet, sustaining serious injuries, including losing consciousness for about 20 minutes. A nearby member of Portland Mountain Rescue witnessed the accident and reported it by cellphone. Assisting climbers were able to relocate the subject to a safer location and provide first aid. A rescue team lowered Creager to an awaiting snowcat, which provided transport to a waiting helicopter in the parking lot.

Analysis

Soft snow conditions can cause loss of footing and also make self-arrest difficult. Roped travel is suggested in such conditions, as it provides the security of a belay or team arrest. (Source: Jeff Sheetz, Portland Mountain Rescue)

FALLING ROCK, POOR CONDITIONS – LATE IN SEASON
Oregon, Mount Hood, Sandy Glacier Headwall

On June 28 Chris Haskins (27) and his partner were ascending the Sandy Glacier Headwall route on Mount Hood when Haskins was struck by a falling rock and suffered a fractured femur. His partner relocated him to a safer area and descended to report the accident. Haskins was air evacuated by an Army Blackhawk helicopter with ground assistance by Portland Mountain Rescue.

Analysis

Like most routes on Mount Hood, the Sandy Glacier Headwall is recommended (safe) only early in the season - typically March-April. These climbers were about two months too late for safe conditions this year. Out of state climbers should check on climbing conditions with the USFS or other local resources if they are not familiar with route conditions. (Source: Jeff Sheetz, Portland Mountain Rescue)

STRANDED – LEADING TO EXHAUSTION AND DEHYDRATION
Oregon, Smith Rocks, Monkey Face

On Tuesday, July 14, 2009, Samuel Wilson (18) and his friend (17), both from the state of Washington, called 911 at 6:30 p.m. They had been climbing routes all day at Smith Rock State Park and had become stranded about 100 feet below a popular feature known as Monkey Face and about 250 feet above an access trail.

Their rope had become stuck and they were exhausted and stranded on a ledge. Twenty-seven Members of the Deschutes County Sheriff's Search and Rescue Unit assembled and set up a Command Post. Six members of the SAR Mountain Rescue Unit established a position in an area known as the "Springboard" and lowered a member of their Team to assess the young climbers' situation on the ledge.

The two climbers were then attached to a rescue rope system and lowered approximately 250 feet to the trail below. The climbers were met at this location and treated at the scene. They were then escorted down the trail and transported by raft across the Crooked River to the SAR Command Post.

Analysis

Local climbers guiding at Smith Rock State Park suggest that young climbers study traditional self-rescue techniques. The climbers had become exhausted and de-hydrated on a very warm day in the Central Oregon desert. Their chosen route on the rock was in the direct sun. Smith Rock regulars often pick their sport routes of the day with sun or shade in mind. (Source: Robert Speik)

OVERDUE – DID NOT RETURN, UNKNOWN CAUSE OF FALL
Oregon, Mount Hood, Sandy Glacier Headwall

On early Friday morning, December 11, Luke Gullberg, (26), Anthony Vietti, (24), and Katie Nolan (29) left Timberline for a climb of the Sandy Glacier Headwall. Their climber registration stated an expected return of 1400 later that day. The form indicated that the party was carrying adequate equipment including a cellphone, but no radio distress beacon (neither PLB nor Mount Hood Mountain Locator Unit).

Concerned friends reported the party overdue on Friday afternoon and Clackamas County Sheriff's Office requested a ground search by Portland Mountain Rescue volunteers at first light on Saturday morning. Searchers were greeted by storm conditions with light snowfall, light winds and limited visibility on the approach to the Sandy Glacier. The first search team dropped down from Illumination Saddle onto the upper Reid Glacier and immediately discovered the body of Luke Gullberg at the 9,200-foot elevation. He appeared to have fallen (unroped) from the headwall above the glacier. An immediate search in the vicinity revealed a helmet, seat harness, glove, camera and two water bottles. Gullberg was clad with only light clothing and neither pack nor climbing tools were found. He was wearing crampons, one of which had apparently become detached during the fall. The searchers now focused their efforts on the headwall and upper glacier area, but were limited by 50-yard visibility and by potential avalanche hazards of soft slab.

The moderate storm continued throughout the day depositing several inches at Timberline Lodge and prevented air search operations. The storm continued and increasing avalanche hazard prevented ground searchers from deployment on Sunday. However, a local NOAA weather forecaster predicted the possibility of temporary clearing late Sunday morning, justifying a request for air search assets. A Blackhawk helicopter from Salem was manned with additional spotters and accumulated several hours of flighttime searching the upper Reid Glacier and headwall area. There was no sign of the remaining missing climbers.

Stormy conditions extended through Monday, but several hours of clear and low winds allowed renewed air searching. This effort included the upper section of the headwall, the summit area, and the Southside descent route. A ground team was able to perform some limited searching in the area around Illumination Saddle and west crater rim. A FLIR-equipped Jayhawk (USCG) was also used, but no signs were detected.

Due to the onset of the winter storm cycle, a thorough ground search could not be conducted for the missing Vietti and Nolan. When the search effort resumes in the spring, it is likely that additional clues will be found. This accident received significant media coverage and brought to the public's mind [once again] two controversies: who should pay for mountain rescues and should (radio locator) beacons be required safety equipment for Mount Hood climbers. It is likely that county and state legislators will again be addressing these issues "for the benefit of the public".

Analysis

The camera found with Gullberg provided some clues of the party's action on Friday morning. It appears that they descended to the 8,500-foot crossover point on Yokum Ridge. Here a decision was made to abandon the Sandy Glacier headwall. Instead the party ascended the lower Yokum ridge. Below the first gendarme, the party traversed to the right crossing Leuthold's Couloir below the hourglass. They continued southeast to the Reid Glacier headwall and ascended one of the gullies on the headwall.

For the steeper climbing the party was roped, with Gullberg in the lead. One of the last pictures showed Gullberg anchored with two self-equalized ice screws, presumably to belay his companions.

It is speculated that there was an accident with an injury to either Vietti or Nolan. As the stronger climber, Gullberg was likely descending the route to get help when he himself was injured during a fall. However, his injuries were severe enough to halt his travel and subsequently he succumbed to hypothermia.

A meaningful analysis cannot be conducted with the current unknowns of the accident. It does not appear that neither route conditions, weather, nor party experience should have an undue contribution to the cause of the accident. (Source: From a report submitted by Jeff Sheetz, Portland Mountain Rescue)

(Editor's Note: A comment on an incident report from last year:

"My name is Devin Lee, the son of Dr. Gary Lee, who was in the [Mount Hood] story [on page 64] in the 2009 ANAM. ... a few minor details: the rock hit my father in the head [not on the back].

"...the most important comment [is that] we knew the conditions. We had climbed late-season before. We knew it was dangerous as soon as we got to the Cooper Spur. My father has climbed that mountain more than 40 times, on all routes, and experience is not a question. Our choice of not wearing helmets was not because we did not fear rock fall. Not only that, we thought we would be out of the rockfall hazards much sooner than that, but the horrible conditions on the upper face of Cooper Spur slowed us down. We had gotten to the top of the snowfield and were very close to Tie-In Rock.

"...We were not ignorant, we were not careless. We went into it with our eyes open, fully aware, taking what precautions we could with conditions that were worse than expected. I don't know what you can do to change anything, since the document is already in print, but I could not, in good conscience, let these thoughts go unsaid."

As I pointed out to Mr. Lee, we are only as good as the information we receive, so sending in first-hand accounts is the best way to go.)

FALL OR SLIP ON ROCK, PROTECTION PULLED OUT
Tennessee, Tennessee Wall, Blood-on-the-Rocks

Fellow climbers and rescue crews evacuated an injured climber on January 25 at the Tennessee Wall after she took a serious leader fall.

Jesse (22) was leading Blood on the Rocks (5.10b/c) in the north section of T-Wall. Witnesses said three or four pieces of gear pulled when she fell, causing her to fall to the ground—about 30-35 feet. The route is an 85-foot, single-pitch.

She had previously fallen on a BD C3 #1 and it held fine. She attempted the move again and fell, this time with devastating results when the cams pulled out of the crack. However, there was enough tension on each piece to slow her down. Landing on her back resulted in a broken pelvis, wrist, and C2 vertebrate.

Analysis

Always check your gear placements after a fall. Falls move gear and can weaken their position. (Source: From a post on Mountain Project and Aram Attarian)

FALL ON ROCK, LOWERING ERROR – ROPE (TOO SHORT) SLIPPED THROUGH BELAY DEVICE (GRIGRI)
Utah, Pine Creek Canyon

On May 9th, rescuers responded to a climbing accident near the Zion-Mount Carmel Tunnel. A 27-year-old man was on a route known as "Feast of Snakes," which is located on the Pine Creek Canyon wall directly below the Zion-Mount Carmel Tunnel, when the fall occurred.

He had placed an anchor at the top of the route and was cleaning gear while being lowered by his partner, who was using a Grigri, at the bottom of the climb. The rope was too short for the slingshot belay technique and the end of the rope went through the Grigri, dropping the climber 20 feet onto his neck and back on a ledge below the route.

Due to the steep terrain and loose footing, along with the mechanism of injury, rescuers called for a helicopter to perform a winch extrication. The rescuers had to do a technical lowering first to move the climber from the ledge. An additional low-angle technical raising, followed by a low-angle lowering, were performed before carrying the patient to an open area away from the canyon walls. A Blackhawk from Nellis Air Force Base extricated the man and flew him to a waiting ambulance at the Coal Pits heli-spot. He was then taken to Dixie Regional Medical Center, where he was diagnosed with C-1, T-1, and T-5 fractures along with a lacerated spleen. About 25 park personnel were involved in the rescue. (Source: From a report by Therese Picard on the NPS Morning Report, May 14, 2009)

Analysis

This is one of several incidents like this during 2009—and for the last several years. It is hard to understand why so many climbers do not have the proper length rope for these situations.

There are those who believe that the Grigri is designed in such a way that it will lock off under these conditions. But obviously that is not so. It is likely that rather than using friction by a good angle with the brake hand, the belayer was using the "clutch" to regulate the speed. This is a common error with the Grigri. (Source: Jed Williamson)

FALL ON ROCK, PROTECTION PULLED OUT
Utah, Big Cottonwood Canyon, Mr. Sandman

A rock climber suffered serious injuries when he fell in Big Cottonwood Canyon on August 4. The 29-year-old man was backing off a route called Mr. Sandman in the Stairs Gulch area, located off Big Cottonwood Canyon Road, when an anchor came out. He fell about 30 feet and landed feet-first on a rock outcropping, apparently breaking both ankles.

Search and rescue crews navigated the very steep, rocky terrain to reach the man, and brought him to an ambulance about two hours after arriving. He was taken to Intermountain Medical Center in Murray. (Source: *The Salt Lake Tribune*, August 5, 2009, and a posting on Mountain Project)

FALLING ICE – GAVE WAY, FALL ON ICE, CLIMBING UNROPED
Utah, Little Cottonwood Canyon, Great White Icicle

On December 31, Gene Rawson (37), a solo ice climber, was near the top of the final pitch of the Great White Icicle. Rawson was waiting for another climber to complete the pitch. Rawson felt he had a firm hold in the ice with his ax. As he was waiting, one of his legs broke through the ice. He shifted weight onto his other foot to pull his leg out when the entire ice section gave way and he fell approximately 300 feet. He reported positive loss of consciousness for unknown length of time and severe left hip pain.

Other climbers in the area witnessed the fall and assisted with the rescue. The Salt Lake County Fire Department paramedics responded with medics from the Little Cottonwood Canyon Fire Station. A backboard was hauled up using a rope system through an anchor set up by the climbers responding to the accident.

Life Flight team assessment: Salt Lake County Sherriff Department notified Life Flight of need for hoist rescue. The team surveyed the scene to determine if hoist rescue could be safely performed. Avalanche risk was deemed minimal due to the lack of snow accumulation on the steep slope: all ice and rock. The victim was located below the anchored belay station at the base of the third pitch. Just out of the drainage upslope and to the east of the Rawson was a moderately-sized flat platform with snow, but no ice in which the hoist paramedic could be safely lowered and prepare the victim for evacuation. Life Flight had communication with EMS on scene and indirectly with the climber responders. The climbers hauled the patient on the backboard up to the flat platform. The medic was inserted via hoist to this location, followed by a vacuum mattress rescue bag to maintain spinal precautions and provide protection from the below freezing temperatures. After the patient was prepared for evacuation (ten minutes), the helicopter returned for hoist evacuation. Mr. Rawson was transported via helicopter to local hospital where he required surgery for a femur fracture. (Source: Carol Rhoades, Flight Nurse, Intermountain Healthcare Life Flight)

Analysis

In an interview with *The Salt Lake Tribune* on January 8, Gene Rawson said trying to climb solo was a mistake. "If I was roped up and had gear in the ice, the chances of anything severe happening would be minimal," he said. "When you go solo, it is taking the sport to the very extreme. It's not a smart thing to do at all, but it is a decision that people make at this level. That is a lesson learned from a lot of people, but being able to live through this, with a 300-foot fall, is huge. Normally, you never hear that someone would live."

The climber, who works for a company in Butte called The Peak that trains Special Forces and other military personnel on rock and ice climbing and mountaineering, praised the work of the Life Flight paramedics who came to his rescue. "It was a great experience to be rescued by these guys," said Rawson. "If it wasn't for them, this would not have gone well. My hats are off to them for everything going as smoothly as it did."

FALL ON ROCK, INADEQUATE PROTECTION
Washington, Columbia Hill State Park, Horsethief Butte

On Sunday April 5, Tony Silva (30), a Gresham Oregon Police Detective, his sister-in-law Laura (26), and her husband, Bobby Silva, along with three young children, planned to set a top rope at Horsethief Butte, a sport climbing area popular with beginning to intermediate climbers from nearby Portland, Oregon, and towns in Washington on the Columbia River.

Horsethief Butte is characterized by many user traces and scrambles climbing up 25 to 50 feet to large ,flat, weathered basalt overlooks. The Park has a "no bolt policy" because of the Native American culturally sensitive nature of this area.

The investigative report and photos show that Tony and Laura were linked together by the system they were constructing. If one fell, the other would be pulled off.

The report stated, "The anchor consisted of two stoppers placed in cracks at the top of the route with three separate loops of grey nylon webbing attached... The middle loop of webbing appeared to be the only loop that had been bearing weight due to all of the knots being weighted... All of the knots in the other two loops (and a third stopper) were non-weighted..." A third stopper was left in place and not attached to the webbing.

Detective Gresham and Laura Silva fell to their deaths from the top of the cliff. The actual fall was not observed.

Analysis

Experience tells us that stopper placement in the typical shallow, worn, narrow, parallel cracks in the flat top of basaltic columns is very insecure. Placements are certainly one directional.

It is believed that one of the climbers was standing or kneeling at the cliff-edge while the other was searching for a placement just below the cliff-edge. When the fall occurred, the anchor was shock-loaded by both climbers and possibly pulled up and out by the climber above.

The Washington State Patrol Investigative Report concludes: "This fall most likely occurred due to human error in building the anchor."

Members of the Mazama climbing club from Portland were also sport climbing nearby. Their monthly print and web publications noted the tragic accident and offered this advice to their readers: "When setting a top-rope or rappel anchor on a cliff-top, a rule of thumb is always secure yourself if you are within two meters of the edge." They suggested that you self-belay by attaching the end of your climbing rope with a locking carabineer to a solid natural or constructed "SERENE" (Secure, Equalized, Redundant, No/Extension) anchor "well back from the cliff", attaching the climbing rope to your harness with a Prusik or Klemheist friction knot looped through a locking carabineer. Of course, traditional practice dictates you should back up your friction knot by tying a figure eight on a bight of the climbing rope a couple of feet below your Prusik loop and clip it to the locker on your harness. The climber should work on the anchor system in the exposed area with a slack-free self-belay.

The Experience Level was described in the Investigative Report as "low intermediate and high intermediate". Both were gym climbers, but neither had much experience in setting traditional anchor systems on basalt columns at Horsethief Butte. (Source: Robert Speik, following interviews with witnesses and study of the Investigative Report and photographs from the Washington State Patrol, Investigative Services Bureau)

FALL ON SNOW – UNUSUAL SLIP
Washington, Mount Shuksan

On May 23, one of two clients sustained an ankle injury when the guide (29) lost his footing on the descent of Mount Shuksan. He slid down a snow slope, and pulled the clients from their stance. Because of snow conditions and gradient, the guide was unable to stop himself before passing the climbers and before the slack in the rope was spent. The total fall was about 400 feet.

Analysis

The guide hadn't set any protection for himself (nor had the other climbers done so as they descended with his belay) because he was on, what was for him, moderate terrain where he felt no danger of losing his footing. It was a very unusual slip—a freak accident—for a skilled guide.

Throughout his career he has guided his clients without error, and he felt terrible about this accident.

The guide commented, "Among many other responsibilities, a guide's job is never to fall. We put in protection on challenging terrain so that if the unexpected happens, ill consequences do not occur or are minimal. We also put in protection on moderate terrain when conditions dictate, such as objective danger or probable difficulty in stopping a slip or a fall by clients. In the case of this accident, we were in open terrain with no objective dangers from above, and I felt secure in my footing. Though the snow was soft, I felt that I could fully control my stance and movement. I have always been conservative in placing protection (especially with clients), and this experience has made me even more so." (Source: Kelly Bush, Wilderness District Ranger, and the guide)

SLIDE INTO STEAM VENT
Washington, Mount Rainier

On May 24th, a climbing guide (age unknown) near the summit of Mount Rainier slid into a steam vent and fell 15 to 20 feet. Climbers with her reported that she had injured ribs on her left side, was experiencing difficulty breathing, and had a reduced level of consciousness. Ranger Chris Olson and two employees from one of the park's guide concessionaires headed out from Camp Muir with a litter and gear for a technical lowering. Rangers David Gottlieb and Jeremy Shank departed Camp Schurman with an oxygen kit. Rangers Philippe Wheelock and Rachel Mueller, having just climbed Fuhrer's Finger, were also directed to the scene.

Her partners, who were part of a commercially guided climb, extricated the climber from the vent. Her injuries turned out to be less severe than first reported. Northwest Helicopters, from Olympia, Washington, provided an MD-530 helicopter, which picked up ranger Phil Edmonds at the park's heli-base with a medical kit and took him to the summit, where they were able to land on the crater rim. The climber was then flown off the mountain and transferred to an ambulance for transport to the hospital. (Source: NPS Morning Report)

Analysis

This is an interesting incident because it suggests snow conditions that may have hidden the vent. There have been very few mishaps of this kind reported. Also of note is that this may have been the first time a helicopter has landed on the summit, according to Ranger Stefan Lofgren in his Annual Report. (Source: Jed Williamson)

FALL INTO CREVASSE
Washington, Mount Rainier, Emmons Flats

On the morning of July 1, Ranger Sam Wick (27) climber Kevin Laney, and I left Camp Schurman around 06:00 for a summit climb. Conditions were excellent with good weather, light winds, and firm snow. Weascended to approximately 12,000 feet where Mr. Laney decided he could not continue ascending the route. Around 10:15, Ranger Wick and Mr. Laney stopped to rest and prepared to descend while I continued ascending toward the summit along with another group of climbers.

About 11:15, I received a radio call from Ranger Wick asking for help at Emmons Flats. However, he did not specify the nature of the incident. At this point I was at 13,500 feet. I was able to make a fast descent on skis to Emmons Flats. Arriving there I did not see Ranger Wick or any other activity, so I continued toward Schurman where I contacted Mr. Laney and was informed that Ranger Wick had not yet come into camp and was last seen above Emmons Flats. At this point I realized Ranger Wick had most likely fallen into a crevasse. I instructed Mr. Laney to return to Schurman, make contact with Anne Keller of International Mountain Guides (IMG), relay to her the situation, and help them assemble rescue and medical gear from the Ranger Hut.

I then started back uphill toward Emmons Flats to look for tracks that would help me locate Ranger Wick. At 11:48, I called park dispatch informing them of the situation and requested 780 (Lofgren) be contacted. I passed an Alpine Ascent International (AAI) group and requested help from their guides. I continued toward the area I thought Ranger Wick would most likely be and found his tracks ending at a crevasse. Around 11:51, I made voice contact with Ranger Wick and was able to approach the crevasse and make visual contact. I saw him lying on the bottom of a crevasse approximately

40 feet deep and 20 feet wide. He was alert and oriented, complaining of a painful and unstable right hip along with pain extending over his right side including ribs, lower back, elbow and both knees. He reported having labored but steady respirations, no external bleeding, no loss of consciousness and no head or neck pain. Based on this information I requested an air evacuation via park dispatch.

The AAI guides came on scene shortly after my initial contact led by senior guide Eric Murphy. I informed them of the situation and they immediately started preparing to lower personnel into the crevasse to further assess and attend to Ranger Wick. Guides Eitan Green and Ben Floyd lowered guides Kjasa Krieger and Eric Murphy into the crevasse. IMG guides Ben Kurdt and Andy Polloczek had come onto the scene around this time and joined the work in progress.

Ms. Keller and Eric Gullickson from IMG arrived on the scene with medical and rescue gear from Schurman. We lowered these supplies into the crevasse along with Ms. Keller and Mr. Green to help with patient care and packaging. Once all the caregivers and equipment were safely in the crevasse, guides Gullickson, Kurdt, Polloczek, and Floyd began preparing a haul system to raise Ranger Wick out of the crevasse.

Around this time I made a phone call to Stefan Lofgren (Park Ranger) informing him that our patient was Sam Wick and gave a detailed report on his condition and of the overall situation. I was informed we would be able to do an air evac with the option of flying directly to the hospital. I then descended to Schurman to collect flight gear, along with additional rescue gear. Once I was back at the scene, the guides attending to Ranger Wick had him packaged and ready for extrication. We hauled Ranger Wick out of the crevasse and he was secured on the surface at 14:43.

Mr. Green and I prepared a landing zone approximately 100 meters away in the Emmons Flats area. Pilot Vince Lopardo with Worldwind Helicopters landed his A-Star on the glacier at 15:51 where Ranger Wick was loaded into the aircraft. I rode in the aircraft attending to Ranger Wick and working as helicopter crewmember. We departed Emmons Flats at 15:53 and flew directly to Harborview Hospital where Ranger Wick was turned over to the emergency department. (Source: Cooper Self, Park Ranger)

Analysis

In the area where Ranger wick skied into the crevasse, the terrain is relatively flat. Indeed, rangers and public commonly walk in this area unroped. Ranger Wick went over in this direction (which was only a few hundred feet off the common route) because the route was generally less broken. Ranger Wick said that he was surprised as he came over a roll to see a crevasse.

The board of review pointed out a few factors that may have contributed to this fall, including splitting up the team near the summit and not remaining in very close contact on the way down. (Source: Stefan Lofgren, Park Ranger, Mount Rainier National Park)

(Editor's Note: It is important to include this narrative and the one preceding it so readers will understand that the possibility of falling into a crevasse on Mount Rainier does not preclude even the most experienced.)

FALL ON STEEP SNOW – UNABLE TO SELF-ARREST, FAULTY USE OF CRAMPONS
Washington, North Cascades National Park, The Triad

On July 1st, Martin Cash (35) and Aaron Zabriskie (26) successfully climbed two of the three summits of a peak known as The Triad. While descending a steep snow slope (~35 degrees), Martin Cash lost his footing and slid approximately 60 feet. The snow was very soft and slushy and he was not able self-arrest. His rapid slide was halted by a rock at the bottom of the snow slope, on a less steep bench. This impact resulted in an open lower leg fracture. This sudden stop likely saved him from tumbling another 100 feet down the steep alp slope and free-falling an additional 200 feet.

Aaron Zabriskie heard Cash yell and went to assist. Zabriskie built a snow anchor for greater security on the slope, thoroughly assessed his friend, and splinted his leg. Zabriskie would go to camp to get overnight gear for Cash, and then he would hike out and alert EMS. As Zabriskie was nearing their camp in Roush Basin (about a mile away) to get the overnight gear, he encountered two North Cascades National Park rangers on a patrol of nearby Eldorado Peak. They quickly initiated a rescue via the park's radio system. Two other rangers responded via helicopter. The initiating rangers were picked up via helicopter and landed below the site. One ranger climbed to the accident site. He re-assessed the patient, site, anchor, and provided radio communication with the climbers.

Due to the steepness of the site and limited options for helicopter landing sites near the climber, two rangers were short-hauled into the site and lifted out the patient in a litter to a flat staging site on a snowfield 600 feet below. Martin Cash was flown out of the backcountry and transferred to a ground ambulance.

Analysis

After reflection, Mr. Cash feels that the accident was definitely preventable by using a more secure technique for descent. He said, "If I had side-hilled down the slope, backing down and plunging my ax when both feet were planted would have prevented it. I think the only lesson [to pass on to others] is to be very careful descending steep snow slopes. Always go face in. Also, my aluminum crampons balled up badly which contributed to me starting the slide."

Backing down a steep, hazardous slope such as this one with or without crampons is much more secure than plunge-stepping or side-hilling. It is also safe and better practice to remove crampons when the snow is starting to ball in them. Also, installing some sort of anti-balling plates on the crampons (or purchasing new ones with plates) can help with this potentially dangerous problem.

Two factors made this a straightforward and expedient rescue. It was extremely fortuitous for Aaron Zabriskie to have made contact with the rangers. Had the timing been different by a few minutes, Martin Cash most likely would have had to spend a night out. Given the clear stable weather, this would have been survivable, but would have increased the risk of infection and tissue damage to Mr. Cash's leg. (Source: Rob Burrows, Climbing Ranger, and Kelly Bush, Wilderness District Ranger)

FALL ON SNOW, FAULTY USE OF CRAMPONS
Washington, Mount Rainier, McClure Rock
On July 4, Mr. Wilkinson (47) was descending the mountain following an Alpine Ascents International (AAI) summit trip. About 2015, Wilkinson tripped over his crampon and fell, with his left knee landing on a picket, resulting in a puncture wound. Guides bandaged the wound and helped him walk down the following morning from approximately McClure Rock at 7,385 feet to Pebble Creek at 7,200 feet. (Source: From a report by Ken Worstell, Park Ranger)
Analysis
It appears that Mr. Wilkinson was climbing alone. The snow conditions were described by Ranger Stefan Wick as "soft," so descending with crampons was not a good idea. (Source: Jed Williamson)

FALLING ROCK — ROCK CAME LOOSE, FALL ON ROCK
Washington, North Cascades — Pickett Range, Mount Terror
Steph Abegg's Narrative: The Picket Range is one of the most rugged areas of the North Cascades. Although the difficulty of the climbing is often moderate, the routes are committing and remote, and any mishap can turn deadly. On July 5, a climbing accident occurred on the North Face of Mount Terror. A member of our climbing party fell, suffering a head injury and broken heel and femur. The injured climber was rescued by National Park Service Rangers before nightfall on July 5, but his uninjured companion was stranded on the North Face for four days in inclement weather.

Mount Terror proved to be aptly named for our party from July 5-9, 2009. There were four of us in the climbing party: Donn Venema (59), Jason Schilling (33), Steve Trent (43), and me (Steph Abegg, 26). All of us are experienced climbers, and have made several previous excursions into the rugged Picket Range. The first three days of our six-day trip had been wildly successful, during which we had climbed the South Face of Inspiration, West McMillan Spire, Degenhardt, and The Pyramid. On Day 4 we started off on our last major climb of our trip: the Stoddard Buttress on the north side of Mount Terror. The Stoddard Buttress is one of the longest and most committing classic lines in the Pickets, and we were excited for the climb.

We left our camp in Crescent Creek at dawn, traversed through the Ottohorn-Himmelhorn col, and reached the base of Mount Terror around 8:00 a.m. It was not long before we began simul-climbing up the buttress, taking a relaxed pace to enjoy what promised to be a sunny and warm summer day in the Pickets. Donn and Jason formed one rope team, and Steve and I formed the other rope team. Steve and I were the leading team.

The accident occurred at 10:30 a.m., shortly after we had traversed around a sharp prow about a third of the way up the route. Steve and I had switched leads and Steve was leading the way up low fifth class ledges back onto the buttress crest. I had just left the belay and begun simul-climbing when I heard a yell above me. I looked up. I think the first thing I saw was a climbing shoe flying through the air. Then, I saw the giant rock and Steve silhouetted against the sky. The next thing I knew I was jerked upwards as Steve hit the end of the rope. He had fallen about 60 feet. Unhurt and surprised, I immediately began calling out to Steve asking him if he was okay. He did not answer me. He was hanging head down at the end of the rope and I was shocked to see quite a bit of blood running down the rock. I yelled to Donn and Jason below. They heard me and began to climb up towards us.

I was able to lower Steve to a ledge and climb up to him. I noticed that the rope attached to Steve was frayed to the core. I was afraid of the potential for the rope to break or slip loose at any time, so I set up additional anchors on some nearby horns. I then maneuvered over to Steve and somehow flipped him so that his head was up. He was still unresponsive, but moaning. His left leg was clearly fractured and he had lost quite a bit of blood from a head wound.

Donn and Jason reached our precarious perch about 15 minutes after the fall. They anchored in and helped to situate Steve to a better position on the small ledge. With his head now fully upright, Steve began to drift in and out of consciousness. Of the three of us, Jason had the strongest first aid skills and he stepped up to the challenge, taking control of addressing Steve's injuries. Under Jason's calm directions, we bandaged Steve's head wound and created a makeshift split for his left leg using the aluminum stay from Donn's pack. Steve began to shiver and display signs of shock, so we layered him with our extra coats. We were encouraged by the fact that Steve tried to help put his arms into the sleeves as we told him what we were doing. He began to be responsive enough to complain of the pain in his leg, and asked repeatedly what had happened.

We had brought along a cellphone to try to call friends and family from the summit. Now, dealing with a serious accident on one of the most rugged spots in the state, this cellphone would be our lifeline. On the previous days, we had been able to get cell service from the summits of both Inspiration and Degenhardt. We agreed that the quickest way to make a call for help would be to continue climbing the buttress to the summit of Mount Terror. We formed a plan. Jason would stay with Steve. Donn and I would continue up towards the summit as quickly (and safely) as we could and try to initiate a helicopter rescue before the night set in. Making the phone call in time was crucial, as Steve's chances of survival would decrease if he had to spend the night on the mountain, especially considering that the deteriorating weather forecast for the coming days.

Donn and I left the accident scene at 12:00 p.m. to simul-climb the rest of the Stoddard buttress to the false summit. When we passed the location of Steve's fall, we saw a large, fresh, dihedral-shaped gash. It is likely Steve had been standing on this section when a sizable chunk of what had appeared to be solid rock tore loose below him. He just happened to be in the wrong place at the wrong time.

As Donn and I simul-climbed towards the summit, we checked repeatedly for cellphone service, but to no avail. When we reached the false summit, we were discouraged that we still could not find a signal. It looked as if we would have to take precious time and climb to the true summit and make one last effort at finding a signal. Then, in a final effort before continuing upwards, Donn found a signal on the far south end of the false summit. At 4:00 p.m., we established contact with 911 and initiated a rescue operation out of the Marblemount Ranger Station. It is scary to realize how critical this call was to getting Jason and Steve off of the mountain alive. About an hour later we were able to call and talk directly to the rangers before they departed in a helicopter to locate Steve and Jason. Shortly after, that we descended to our camp in Crescent Creek Basin.

Rescuer's Narrative: At 16:06 the North Cascades National Park Communications Center in Marblemount received the report of Donn Venema's call via Skagit County 911. A helicopter was put on standby and SAR rangers were notified. Rangers Kelly Bush and Kevork Arackellian flew reconnaissance of the incident site with HiLine Helicopters pilot Jason Moorhead. Steve and Jason were located at 17:57 and it was quickly decided that this would require a short-haul rescue. However, due to the severity of the terrain and local turbulent winds, pilot Moorhead declined to fly this particular short-haul mission. Upon this decision, Bush radioed from the helo for Comm Center to contact both pilot Anthony Reece, as well as first notification to Whidbey Naval Air Station, for the consideration of their involvement. Pilot Reece responded and flew the second recon with Bush and Arackellian. On this flight, a short-haul staging site was chosen above the climber's camp in Crescent Creek Basin. Bush was dropped off there and briefed Donn and Steph on the situation, leaving them an NPS radio.

The helicopter returned to a staging area near Newhalem, took on fuel and the short-haul rigging. During this time, it was decided that there was likely only enough daylight for one short-haul maneuver. The helicopter returned to Crescent Creek Basin where Ranger Arackellian attached to the short-haul line at 20:25. Steve was plucked from the Stoddard Buttress at 20:30 and flown directly to the Newhalem helipad. This was an approximate ten-minute flight, with Arackellian attempting to hold Steve in a stable position while both hung 100 feet below the helo. Ranger Cori Conner directed medical care of Steve at Newhalem until 21:17 when an Airlift NW medical helicopter arrived. Steve was transferred to flight nurse care and taken to a hospital in Bellingham, WA.

During the three day period of waiting for clear weather to fly Jason out, his spirits were bolstered at his bivy by regular check-ins on the radio, which included the opportunity to talk briefly with loved ones. Concern for Jason's emotional health grew each day, as he was forced to stay put on a ledge through rain and snowstorms, hoping for a rescue, but knowing it would not come as long as he was shrouded in clouds. During this time media interest and outside pressure to complete the rescue grew as well.

On the morning of July 9 the SAR team was prepared for either a short-haul or a climbing-based evacuation. The weather forecast was uncertain for that day. While there was no forecast for precipitation, the partly cloudy forecast could have meant either partial clearing around the high peaks or them remaining shrouded in the clouds. Rangers Erin McKay and Rob Burrows from North Cascades NP and Rangers Philippe Wheelock and Rachel Muehler from Mount Rainer National Park readied to be inserted via helicopter below the cloud level to climb to Jason and descend with him. However, at 09:09 the weather appeared to clear enough for a short-haul attempt. They backed off the first attempt because of uncertain cloud level, but soon after a second successful attempt was made. Jason was short-hauled to the staging site and then flown inside the helicopter to the Newhalem area staging site, arriving at 10:08.

Analysis

All members of this party are strong climbers with experience in the North Cascades range, including trips into the Picket Range. These routes are known for their unsavory approaches, remote location, and committed routes. They all agree that this accident was being at the wrong place at the wrong time and was not preventable unless they did not climb the route. All agree that Steve is a careful climber versed in testing holds on less than solid rock. It seems there was no obvious sign of the instability of the rock that calved off. This incident is a powerful reminder that the risk of death and/or injury from objective hazards is clear and real when climbing in the mountains. Climbers can be high caliber in skills and character, but this does not insure safety. Mount Terror has been shedding rock and ice for millions of years and it is in the laws of probability that sometimes we are in the way. Climbers must be willing to assume this risk, which is beyond human control. "Sometimes bad things just happen in spite of our best efforts to avoid them," as Donn Venema said.

If they had been belaying pitches instead of doing a running belay, Steve's fall might have been shorter, but it might not have prevented the injuries. Also they would have been climbing twice as slow, a significant risk in and of itself on such a long route.

Another life-saving decision was to simul-climb on a 60 meter, doubled over, small diameter rope. In the fall, one of the strands of rope was completely severed with the other damaged to the core. Had the party been using a single strand, this could have resulting in both members of the rope team taking a very long fall.

The role of the cellphone was crucial to initiating a rescue on that last day of good weather and likely saved Steve's life. Having knowledge of where the cellphone would work and managing use so that there was the possibility of a call was important. Had Steph and Donn headed down instead of ascending further up Mount Terror, the phone call connection would not likely have worked. Cellphone coverage on top of some of the summits in the southern Picket Range is a new phenomenon in the last few years and there are still many, many places in the North Cascades where there is no coverage.

When asked to reflect on the incident, Donn Venema provided a lengthy narrative. His final paragraph is quoted here:

"We were very lucky to have been climbing in a team of four. Steph has said she is not sure what she would have done had Jason and I not been there. I'm not sure what I would have done in that situation either, but I think it would have probably come down to leaving Steve alone and either rappelling the face or, more likely in this case, soloing to the top in hopes of making a cell call. In either case, leaving Steve alone would have been extremely dangerous for him, not to mention very difficult emotionally for the partner leaving him. And obviously, climbing alone either up or down on technical terrain to go for help carries its own risk. I would never recommend to any climber that they always climb in larger groups, but, especially in remote areas, there's no question that numbers increase your safety should there be an accident, and that fact is something that climbers should at least consider. Even though I've done the vast majority of my climbing as a party of two, and will continue to do climbs as a party of two, I've become more conservative in recent years and tend to prefer the safety of having more bodies around as we get farther and farther from civilization. If this incident has had any effect on how I climb in the future, it is probably to reinforce that preference." (Source: From Steph Abegg's narrative and Kelly Bush, North Cascades Wilderness District Ranger, and the rangers who were on the rescue)

BLOCK OF ICE CALVED OFF – FALL ON ICE
Washington, North Cascades National Park, Torment-Forbidden Traverse

On August 9, AMGA Instructor Pool member, Certified Rock Guide and former member of the AMGA Board of Directors, Craig Luebben (49), died of injuries sustained while attempting to climb the Torment-Forbidden Traverse. Craig and Willie Benegas were climbing and training together for an upcoming AMGA Alpine Exam at the time of the incident.

They started the traverse on the SE Face of Torrent via the Taboo Glacier. At the bergschrund, with Craig leading and Willie belaying, Craig attempted to bypass the remnant ice hanging above the berg-schrund by ascending rock on the right and then traversing left on to the ice for the exit moves. According to Wille, around 0630, as Craig transitioned from the rock to the ice, a block of ice 100 feet by 20 feet by ten feet calved off, taking Craig with it, resulting in a 30-40-foot fall. A single cam device held his fall. While not struck by the initial block, Craig was critically injured by falling ice and debris as he hung from his rope. Willie managed to get Craig to his belay stance in the berg-schrund, stabilize and treat his injuries and contact rescue personnel. Despite Willie's heroic efforts and a swift response from NCNP SAR personnel, Craig succumbed to his injuries.

Willie suffered minor injuries to his leg and is expected to make a full recovery. (Source: From an AMGA posting and a report by Kelly Bush, Wilderness District Ranger)

(Editor's Note: There was one other report from the North Cascades that came directly from two climbers, 43 and 50, one of whom momentarily lost control on a rappel, resulting in a fractured seventh rib. The climber thinks that if he had been using an autoblock, he might have been able to use is hands to avoid hitting the ledge with his back when he lost his balance. This is a good observation in general.)

BOLT HANGER "FAILURE", FALL ON ROCK
Washington, Index, Upper Town Wall

While climbing the route "Calling Wolfgang" on the Upper Town Wall at the Sport Wall area I took a 40-50 fall nearly hitting the ground. My fall was the result of not one but two bolt hanger failures. After climbing to the third bolt approximately 45 feet up, I weighted the bolt with body weight to clean holds and scout pro placements above. Upon weighting the bolt, I immediately popped away from the cliff as the hanger broke. To my surprise, I continued to fall as the second bolt hanger broke as well. I scraped against a small ledge and came to a stop a few feet above the ground. Bruised and well scraped up but not broken. Very lucky.

If anyone is considering climbing routes on this wall, proceed with caution. This was my first trip up any of the routes on the Sport Wall and I have no idea what the condition of any other bolts may be. I encourage folks to spread the word about the possible condition of old bolts at Index (or elsewhere for that matter). Keep in mind this hanger failed under BODY WEIGHT. (Source: A posting on Mountain Project, no name provided)

Analysis

Matt and I went and climbed Lovin' Arms yesterday late afternoon. So we arrive at the base to meet two climbers who have just had a near-death experience on a route left of there. ...the guy claimed to have fallen and broken TWO bolt hangers, nearly decking and death. I pointed out that the best part of a near-death experience was the "near" part. He looked to have cut his elbow pretty bad, but fine otherwise. Both he and his partner were pretty freaked out, had been looking for the hangers with no success. He had lowered off the bolt that finally caught him, and a nut he placed below it. On the rap off of Lovin' Arms Matt, and I checked it out and took his draw, runner, and nut. The draw was on an old 3/8-inch bolt that was rusted, but with a hanger that looked fine, labeled "Kong-Bonatti."

I noticed a broken bolt section on the ledge I passed below, carefully, and brought it home. It looks fine externally, the internal looks like rusted cardboard. I'm guessing some sort of old carbon steel hanger coated with zinc or something. Here is a link to photos. Yow! public.me.com/hummer-machine (Source: Another posting on Mountain Project under "dberkinka")

(Editor's Note: There were more incidents reported from Mount Rainier National Park, but not enough detail was available. One involved a skier incurring a fracture above his boot while on the Wilson-Nisqually Glacier divide. Another was a climber who had been hit on the head with a rock near Disappointment Cleaver. A client (36) in a guided party was reported as having shortness of breath and was flown out from Cathedral Gap. This was diagnosed later as an infection, perhaps strep throat. A client (55) in another guided party was reported to have a fractured lower leg. He was evacuated by helicopter from Emmons Shoulder.

In his Annual SAR Report, Ranger Stefan Lofgren indicated that there were no fatalities in the park during the summer and that the incident rate for registered climbers was .02%)

FALL ON ROCK, SEVERED ROPE, PLACED NO OR INADEQUATE PROTECTION, NO HARD HAT
West Virginia, Seneca Rocks, La Bella Vista

On the morning of July 11, Ian Shevill (42) and his partner Brian (20's) were climbing La Bella Vista, a two-pitch 5.10a trad climb, on the East Face of South Peak when he fell to his death. Matthew Lombardi, an Instructor and Guide for the Seneca Rocks Climbing School (SRCS), was witness to the accident and recounts:

Around 10:00 a.m., I was climbing with clients near Ye Gods and Little Fishes and noticed a climbing party of two on La Bella Vista. After some time I heard a grunt, then a bang. I looked over to the climbers on La Bella Vista to see a man falling out of the Skyline Chimney, hitting several ledges as he fell into the trees below.

I noticed a severed climbing rope attached to his harness. I grabbed my radio and called another guide in town and asked him to call 911. I then lowered my client so I could offer assistance to Ian. At the same time, climbers from either side of The Fin who heard the fall were below checking Ian for a pulse. Another guide who was nearby and witnessed the fall was able to tandem-rappel with his client and respond.

Since others had responded to Ian before I could, I gave more information over the radio. I also made contact with Brian. He was okay but shaken up. I told him that others were helping Ian and that he needed to keep himself safe. He managed to rappel to the ground.

Climbers, including two nurses, worked on Ian and after a time realized there was nothing else they could do for him given the severity of the fall and his injuries. (Source: Matthew Lombardi)

Analysis

From what I could tell, Ian was approximately ten feet above his first piece of protection (a #2 Camalot) when he fell, suggesting that the rope severed somewhere between him and his last piece. Somehow his brand-new 60m, 9.4mm rope got caught in a notch and due to the dynamics of the fall, pulled the rope apart. As the belayer, Brian felt almost no "pull" in the fall. The idea of a factor-2 fall with the rope caught in a notch is the best explanation we (climbers and others on the scene) can come up with. Upon inspection, the rope sheath on the cut rope didn't look like it was cut. Instead, it looked as though it was pulled apart.

A 9.4mm rope is a relatively skinny rope for trad climbing at Seneca. Climbers are reminded to watch for sharp edges and any other rock features that could compromise the rope in the event of a fall. Full-length runners and additional protection can help in rope management. Using additional protection may have prevented the rope from getting caught in the notch. A larger diameter rope or double rope technique should also be considered.

Although he was not wearing a helmet, I don't think it would have helped him. One final note, the climbing community came together in an extremely helpful and compassionate way to help a fellow climber. (Source: Matthew Lombardi and a posting by James Curry)

AVALANCHE, WEATHER
Wyoming, Cody, South Fork, Main Vein

To begin, Keith (Spencer, 45) and I drove up to Cody on Thursday, New Year's Day. Having recently soloed Cho Oyu, the world's sixth highest peak, Keith was practically voluble. He talked more in that seven-hour drive than I'd heard him say in the last decade. He was proud and pleased with his approach and performance on Cho Oyu. He'd made close friends on the climb and they were already planning an expedition to Lhotse in two years time. We spent the night in Kenny Gasch's Spike Camp in downtown Cody, rose at five, were scouting falls in the South Fork by seven. After glassing a half dozen falls on both north and south slopes, we decided on the Main Vein, a WI-IV, five-pitch route on the north side near the end of the valley. It was snowing and blustery, usual Wyoming winter conditions. We could see the top headwall double-pitch (220 feet), but little above that because of the inclement weather. We chose this route for several reasons: 1) it looked fat and thus safe; 2) the first pitch, which rarely forms, was in; 3) Keith had never climbed this route before, this would be my fourth ascent; 4) the grade was moderate. I led the ice pitches, Keith led the snow pitches. Part way up the second ice pitch we were hit by a spindrift avalanche and both blasted with snow dust. This is common in the South Fork.

As far as I know, no one has ever died or even been hurt from an avalanche in the South Fork. It is a dry region and avalanches were not previously considered a threat. At the base of the third ice pitch, we found avalanche debris, which surprised us. I suggested that this was a good sign, because it meant that anything loose above us had now slid. Keith didn't respond, but this was typical Keith. Focused on the climbing, he probably hadn't spoken five sentences that day. At the base of the headwall—the fourth and fifth pitches—although it was still snowing and blowing, the icefall and the rock walls around us were clear of snow and there was no evidence of a fresh avalanche, which we took as a good sign. I set off on the fourth pitch at 1:00 p.m., climbed 115 feet and put in a belay, deeply placing two long screws and stomping out a small platform for my feet. I placed the belay in a tiny alcove of ice, below a vertical bulge, so that Keith might be protected from any falling ice when I led the last pitch. Keith seconded methodically, as was Keith's way. He was in high spirits. Cresting the last vertical bulge, he was 15 feet below me, when he shouted, "Avalanche," in a nonchalant voice. I'm sure he expected it to simply be another slough. A millisecond later, a horrific roar began. It was such a hideous, unimaginable thunder that I can only compare it to placing your head against a railroad track as a freight train blasts by. I instinctively squeezed flat against the ice. The bombardment went on and on and I fully expected to be torn from the ice. I was screaming from terror. I cannot say how long the avalanche lasted—30 seconds, a minute, two minutes. When it finally ended, I was still there and Keith was gone.

The power of the avalanche had pulled the entire icy rope through the belay device. Keith had fallen 200 feet. I found him hanging at the end of the rope. He was not breathing and had no pulse and it was clear his neck had been broken. The next day Keith's body was recovered and a search and rescue plane flew by to take photographs of the Main Vein drainage. The avalanche had started when a cornice at the crest of the mountain, 1,500 feet above Keith and I, broke. The crown face of the avalanche was 5-10 feet deep and extended a quarter mile along the mountaintop. Thousands of tons of snow funneled through a 30-wide passage. There is no reason this massive avalanche slid at this moment. It could have slid that night, or two days earlier or two days later. Keith and I had no knowledge of this cornice, but I later learned that high winds and very cold temperatures had created a dramatically unstable snowpack. I don't know why the ice screws held. There is no reason I am alive and Keith is dead. Keith was a man of extraordinary honor, humility and discipline. I will miss him terribly, as will we all. (Source: Mark Jenkins)

FALL ON SNOW – NEAR MISS
Wyoming, Grand Teton National Park, Mount Moran, Skillet Glacier

On June 2nd, a woman (20+) was ascending the Skillet Glacier with her male friend with intentions of skiing the Skillet Col. Both were wearing backpacks with skis on their packs, no helmets, unknown if they had crampons and axes, but I'm guessing they did. Near the top of the Skillet the woman lost her footing or fell backwards. She tumbled 1,200 feet down the Skillet, a fall that is commonly referred to as "Tomahawking." There were two other skiers at the top that were waiting for her and her friend to top out before they began their decent. They were already in their skis as they saw her fall. One of the two skied down to her right away to assess her injuries. She was beat up but able to ski out on her own and didn't report the incident. Occasionally we hear about some spectacular near-miss incident days later and never hear anything more. This information was relayed to me in rumor format, so I don't know any more than that. (Source: Chris Harder, GTNP Ranger)

(Editor's Note: Spectacular slides down the Skillet Glacier used to be an annual event, especially popular among young people working summer jobs at the various

concessions. Thanks to an education program, these events are now infrequent. But when they happen, they are worth mentioning and becoming part of the orientation for seasonal workers.)

FALL ON ROCK – INADEQUATE BELAY, MISCOMMUNICATION
Wyoming, Lander, Sinks Canyon, Scud Wall

Chelsea Jackson (20) was sport climbing on the Scud Wall in Sinks Canyon on June 21 when this incident occurred. She had recently met her climbing partners, Garrett Newcomer and Christina Locastro, at her new job at Jackson Lake Lodge.

About 3:00 p.m., Jackson cleaned their gear off of the anchor at the top of Banoffee (5.10a). She never asked for the belay to be changed while she was cleaning the anchor. Her belayer, Newcomer, unsuccessfully tried to communicate to her that he was taking her off of belay. When she re-weighted the rope, she fell approximately 50 feet while her belay rope zinged through the top anchor, she bounced off the ground in a seated position, then she rolled down the steep slope below.

Newcomer said that, "We told her she was off belay when she tied into the anchor, but she never responded. I let go of the rope, a few minutes went by, then she screamed and fell right next to us, landing on her hip before she rolled down the hill." Newcomer said he thinks she never realized she was ever off belay and that he expected her to get off belay while clipped in, and then ask for a new belay before she descended.

Jackson was taken to the hospital and treated for a dislocated hip, bruised lung, and mild whiplash. At the time of her interview a month post-accident, she had returned to work waiting tables and was climbing again.

Analysis

Jackson later concurred that she never realized she was ever off belay and was shocked when she started falling after unclipping herself from the anchor.

While her injury was quite serious, two similar falls in Sinks Canyon have resulted in much more severe injuries. Possible mitigating factors for Jackson's fall included: 1) friction from the belay rope zinging through the anchor (two rings spaced about 6 inches apart), and 2) Jackson landing on a very steep slope which redirected her kinetic energy—akin to a ski jumper landing on the outrun.

Lessons learned: This was a "normal accident" (Charles Perrow, *Normal Accidents: Living with High-Risk Technologies*, 1984) involving human error and a failed redundant pathway.

The climber (not the belayer) is the one who initiates the belay being taken off, no matter what the belayer expects the climber to do. Also, the belayer should not let go of the rope unless the climber specifically asks to be taken off of belay. These two standards are universal. While it is certainly common for groups of climbers to develop their own routines for how they handle belays for lowering or rappelling off of anchors, these routines need to be communicated clearly. But human error happens, which is why high-risk systems often include redundancy.

Jackson pointed out that she could have thwarted this accident if she had communicated with the belayer before weighting the rope for getting lowered. This type of redundancy in critical communication can prevent a fall like this, no matter what belay routine is being used for cleaning anchors. (Source: John Gookin, SAR Commander, FCSO)

SLIP ON SNOW – UNABLE TO SELF-ARREST, OFF-ROUTE, NO HARD HAT, INEXPERIENCE
Wyoming, Grand Teton National Park, Mount Teewinot, Northwest Couloir
On July 11, Sam Russell (22) fell approximately 200 vertical feet down the Northwest Couloir of Teewinot, sustaining significant injuries. The fall resulted from a slip on snow that occurred at the top of the NW Couloir just below the prominent "V-notch" near the summit of Teewinot at about 12,000 feet of altitude. He was unable to self-arrest in the snow, sliding and falling some 100 feet. He then impacted rock and fell approximately another 100 feet over rock, coming to rest in a steep alcove just below a large rock block. Three companions witnessed the fall.

They split into two parties, one descending skiers' right of the gully (N. Evon and D. Ozment) and the other descending skiers' left (S. Reece and S. Russell). Reece assisted Russell with the crampons and began to descend. Reece slipped on the hard snow, but was able to self-arrest. He then moved skiers' right over to where Evon and Ozment were descending. Russell then began to descend. He was not wearing a helmet.

About 1130, Russell slipped at the same location as Reece, but was unable to self-arrest, despite several attempts. After about 50 feet, he began to tumble and cartwheel. After another 50 feet, he impacted rock, and continued his fall over steep rock for another 100 feet. He finally came to rest in a steep alcove just below a large rock block.

Ozment climbed down to Russell and assisted him as best he could while Evon contacted Grand Teton Dispatch via a cellphone call to his girlfriend (who relayed the information to GRTE Dispatch). Reece and Evon remained about 100 feet above the accident site, where they were able to communicate with the Rescue Cache using a cellphone. SAR Coordinator R. Johnson received the initial call and established contact with Reece. Johnson then turned over rescue coordination to G. Montopoli so that he could assist with the helicopter component of the operation.

The rescue got under way. One ranger was flown to a spot where he could climb to the accident site. Three other rangers where flown to a heli-site.

Russell was immobilized on a backboard and extracted. They arrived at Lupine Meadows about 1430. He was transported to St. John's Hospital via Medic. At St. John's Hospital, Russell was diagnosed with a left orbital fracture, lacerated spleen, left tibia fracture, trauma to both knees and chin, and other injuries.

At the accident site, Rangers Jernigan and Vidak assisted Russell's three companions from their locations on technical ground in the NW Couloir to the helispot. They were then flown down by helicopter to the Lupine Meadows Rescue Cache.

Analysis

They had left Lupine Meadows Parking Area at about 0300 hours and as- cended the East Face route of Teewinot. They arrived at the summit about 0900. They intended to descend the Southwest Couloir; however, when they arrived at the V-notch, about 200 feet below and to the southeast of the Teewinot summit, they were unaware of the need to ascend up and over a ridge into the next gully, which leads to the SW couloir. They therefore began a descent into the Northwest Couloir, putting them off-route.

Russell was completely inexperienced with climbing on steep snow/ice and using an ice ax and crampons. (Source: Ranger George Montopoli— Incident Commander, Investigating Ranger)

FALLING ROCK – FAILURE TO TEST HOLDS
Wyoming, Wind River Range, Cirque of the Towers

On August 1, while ascending Pingora Peak, Kelsey Dayton pulled a large rock off while following Joe Kelsey up a 4th-class chimney. The rock grazed her helmeted head then broke her left humerus.

Analysis

Mid-altitude mountaineering in this location has significant loose rock hazards due to freeze/thaw cycles. (Source: John Gookin, SAR Commander, FSCO)

FALL ON ROCK, INADEQUATE PROTECTION – FAILURE TO BRING RACK, FAILURE TO TURN BACK – WEATHER
Wyoming, Grand Teton National Park, East Face of Mount Teewinot

On August 16 about 0500, Brian Barwatt (31) and I (Van Roberts, 22) de- parted the Lupine Meadows trailhead for a traverse of Teewinot to Mount Owen. We had been climbing in the area for about a week and had gotten up the East Ridge of Wolf's Head III—5.6, the Northeast Face of Pingora IV—5.8, and the Complete Exum Ridge on the Grand Teton IV in a day. We also climbed The Snaz IV—5.9. We had spoken to a ranger at the Jenny Lake Ranger Station regarding our intended route and felt comfortable with it. The climbing is rated 5.4 at the hardest, with most of the route being

4th class and scrambling. Due to the lack of technical difficulty, we elected to bring no protection with us. Instead, we brought a single 8mm rope and our harnesses and belay devices for rappels we were to encounter along the ridge connecting the mountains.

The night prior to our departure, the mountains were completely enveloped in clouds, and a steady rain fell on our car at the trailhead. When we departed the next morning, the mountains were still hidden in clouds. As we climbed the trail, we eventually broke through the clouds, and were able to see Teewinot's East Face above us, covered in newly fallen snow. Progressing upwards, we encountered more snow—approximately 3-4 inches in some spots. Because we had anticipated these conditions, we brought crampons, ice axes, and wore mountaineering boots. We began the ascent of the face with a snowfield to the climber's right of the Idol and Worshiper towers. The face was icy and snowy in many places and there was little dry rock to be found due to the melting snow. We were not familiar with the route, but we believed we were following the general path of ascent. Some sections of what we believed was the route had to be bypassed by sketchy face-climbing on wet rock, which we did unroped. Eventually, we made it to a gully, near what looked like the summit. The gully was severely iced, with chunks of ice periodically clattering down on us.

At this point, I expressed to my partner my discomfort with the conditions. I told him that I was tired, to the point where I was worried I would make a careless mistake. He offered to lead on our rope and belay from above. I agreed to continue on. He pulled a difficult face move to the left of the gully on wet rock and then belayed me up, anchored to some fixed webbing he had found. He had lowered the rope to me. I had clipped a figure-8 on a bight into a locking carabiner around my belay loop. I offered to lead up the next pitch, climbed up a short distance, felt uncomfortable with the terrain, and climbed back down, offering him the lead. He led through the moves I was uncomfortable with and continued onward. At one point, he paused before a face section, and later revealed to me he had thought it looked difficult, and had considered retreating, but climbed on. He anchored himself via a loop of rope over a horn. As he was creating his anchor, I pulled a pair of dry gloves out of my pack, and also put on my climbing helmet, which I had not been wearing up to this point. He belayed me up to his anchor. The terrain above looked relatively easy, so I continued upward. I had almost all the rope out and was searching for a horn to sling for an anchor. I saw nothing, but above me, past a bulge, was a ledge, which I felt would most likely hold some prospect for an anchor. I was working through the moves on the bulge, which was awkward and wet, when my foot unexpectedly popped off a hold, causing me to slip. I hit a ledge immediately, and stopped for a moment. I felt relief briefly, until I began to slide. I panicked, and began trying to grab any hold I could on the face I was sliding down. I yelled to my partner, "Falling!" and began to pick up speed, tumbling down the face. I thought to myself, "Oh my god, this is how I die," and then waited for it to happen. I saw and heard my ice ax, which I had stashed between my back and my pack flying down the face. I continued to fall, impacting ledges until my fall was suddenly arrested.

I hung from the rope, disoriented. My climbing partner asked if I was ok, and I replied that I was alive. I saw a ledge on my left accessible by a move of 4th -class. In my mind, I was worried that whatever had caught me would break and that I needed to get to the ledge and sit down. I unclipped from the rope and threw my pack down to my partner, thinking that it would cause me to be off balance. I could not see very well, but managed to cross the face to the ledge and sit down. After I collected myself, I clipped back into the rope, and climbed down to the belay. My partner stated he believed the fall to be about 70 feet. As I sat on the ledge at the belay, my partner climbed up and freed the rope, which had caught on a very small horn that held my fall.

I felt dazed and my vision was blurry. As a paramedic student, I tried to assess myself for possible injuries. My right glove had been torn off in the fall and I had multiple abrasions to that hand and abrasions to both palms. My arms were also abraded and I could feel other cuts on my legs. My right hip was very painful and my left hamstring rebelled whenever I tried to weight it. My helmet (Petzl Meteor III) had multiple dents in it and the band used for adjusting size on the back was broken. I had pain and what I believed was an abrasion on my left posterior skull and bilateral posterior rib pain on inspiration. I palpated my cervical spine and found no tenderness.

My partner arrived back at the belay and was able to lower me down to less technical terrain. As I waited on the ledge, my vision became progressively blurrier. We continued a system in which we would scramble down, finding a pinch or horn tie off the rope, thus allowing me to rappel on a single strand. My partner would then untie the rope and down-climb to my next location. On one of my rappels, I found my ice ax, and gave it to my partner to carry. We continued this until we arrived at the lower snowfield. I rappelled to the end of the rope, but was still on the snowfield. I was able to kick out a large enough platform to allow my partner to down-climb to me and hand me my ice ax, which I was then able to use to descend the rest of the snow. My vision had returned to almost normal and I was able to slowly hike the trail back down to the car, uneventfully.

On the way to St. John's ER, my vision began to blur again. After being admitted to the ED, I was released with only a minor head injury, in addition to my various scrapes and contusions.

Analysis

In retrospect, we made a number of decisions that contributed to this fall and I was incredibly lucky that the rope caught a knob on my way down.

This incident could have easily been prevented by a few factors. Had we listened to our gut feelings and turned around, this would not have happened. The conditions were less than ideal, but wet rock, ice, and snow are frequently encountered in the mountains and part of climbing, in my opinion, is being able to travel safely in these situations.

We were not exceeding our climbing abilities; however, our decision to leave the rack in the car created a hazard that resulted in a long, potentially injurious fall. Considering the new snow and ice present up high and the change this presented, taking gear would have been a prudent decision. Also, I am very thankful that our rope held. In an effort to cut weight, we took a single twin rope. I had researched the holding power of a single twin rope and had read that they would hold one fall, rated appropriately by the UIAA, as long as the rope was not loaded over an edge. Obviously, it did hold.

Also, I put my helmet on almost as an afterthought. This is rare for me, especially in the mountains, as I usually wear it constantly. It undoubtedly saved my life. (Source: Van Roberts)

FALLING ROCK – FALL ON ROCK, INADEQUATE PROTECTION, FAILURE TO TURN BACK
Wyoming, Grand Teton National Park, Death Canyon, Caveat Emptor

On August 29, Brian Huff (23) was leading the second pitch of Caveat Emptor and established an anchor at the top in what is considered the normal belay location. (A small ledge and alcove approximately 170 feet up and left from the first belay.) It is believed that Huff used a long yellow sling (1-inch webbing) to wrap a large block setting on the climber's left side of the belay ledge. It was also stated by Jonathon L, his partner, that Huff also placed a tri-cam as part of the anchor. Jonathon stated that Huff pushed and shoved on the block and it was solid. It is likely that Huff clipped into this same sling with his harness daisy chains as his personal attachment point.

Jonathon followed the second pitch up to the large roof, cleaning the protection as he went. He fell trying to pull up over the lip of the roof and reported "tweaking his wrist" slightly during the fall. He decided that he did not want to finish the climb and asked Huff to lower him. Due to communication difficulties, Jonathon got lowered only a few feet. Huff was using a Petzl Reverso as his belay device. It was in the "auto lock" mode. In order to lower Jonathon, he attached a long cordelette to the rope as a prusik and established a small raising system to break the rope free from the device. It is likely that after lowering a short distance the device locked up again.

Jonathon then decided that he could ascend the rope if it were fixed to the anchor and asked his partner to do this. Jonathon reported that they had very clear communication on this point and Huff said that the rope was fixed to the anchor. Jonathon began to ascend the rope using a Cinch device. He went up about ten feet. He said the rope started to slide slowly down, so he decided that he would try to climb the route instead. Huff then used the prusik cord to transfer the weight off of the fixed knot and onto his belay device, now rigged on his harness. He did not complete the load transfer.

At this point it is believed that the block that was serving as the main anchor became dislodged and was pulled from the ledge. Due to the position of the block on the ledge, it is likely that the block fell from the ledge and then pulled Huff off as well. The last piece of protection that he had placed while leading was a BD .5 cam-a-lot approximately 25-30 feet below the belay anchor. He likely took a tumbling "head first" fall down and to climber's right. He fell approximately 40-50 feet, being stopped by the rope through the .5 cam-a-lot and the counter balance weight of Jonathon on the other end of the rope.

At the same time, Jonathon was trying to determine what was going on when he free fell 30-40 feet, being stopped by the rope approximately 20 feet above the first belay ledge. He said rocks of various sizes falling past him, but luckily did not hit him. (Witnesses at the base of the climb reported the largest of these rocks being "microwave-sized." It is believed that this rock was the block that Huff had slung as the anchor.) To clarify, both climbers were now hanging on their respective ends of the rope, anchored only by the .5 cam-a-lot. Huff is still above the roof out of sight of his partner.

Huff suffered several injuries including a concussion, laceration above his left eye, and a severely dislocated left shoulder. It is unknown if he lost complete consciousness, but it is believed he did for a short time at least.

After recovering from the fall, Huff rigged his end of the rope and began rappelling down towards Jonathon. It is believed that he had to re-arrange various items contained in the anchor rigging, which was now tangled at his location. He did not place another anchor and began rappelling on the counter balance weight of Jonathon on the other end of the rope. Huff had just enough rope on his end to barely reach the first belay anchor, passing his partner en route.

Two Exum guides had heard the accident and climbed up to the first belay. They assisted in clipping Huff into the anchor and reported the accident via cellphone. Luckily the knot that Huff had used to fix the rope to the anchor ended up on the opposite side of Jonathon and jammed into the carabiner at the .5 cam-a-lot. Huff came off of the rope and his partner remained hanging on the other end of the rope. Luckily, due to the knot jammed into the carabiner, he did not fall any further.

Jonathon was trailing a second rope, which the Exum guides were able to reach. They then had Jonathan tie into this rope and they belayed him while he down-climbed to the first belay anchor. The Exum guides then lowered him down to the first large ledge on the climb and assisted his partner in rappelling to the same ledge. They bandaged Huff's head laceration and made him as comfortable as possible.

I arrived on scene approximately an hour later (on foot) and performed a full assessment, applied oxygen, established an IV, and splinted his arm/shoulder. The decision was made to short-haul Huff from this ledge. A litter was inserted first, followed by Ranger Guenther. Huff was placed in full c-spine precautions in the litter and short-hauled from the ledge, attended by Ranger Guenther.

Huff spent the rest of the evening in the hospital undergoing tests and evaluations. His shoulder was reduced without surgery and no fractures were found. He was released that night.

Analysis
Notable details:

The tri-cam was never located. It is possible it fell into the crack and may be jammed there.

The rope (9.4mm) had several abrasions to the sheath, but remained intact.

Based on the debris left on the belay ledge and the scrape marks, it is believed that the block used for the anchor was just sitting on the slightly down sloping ledge and was not attached to the main cliff. There was no evidence of any recent fracturing.

There are cracks of various sizes at the belay ledge that appeared would have accepted a variety of protection in different size ranges.

The .5 cam-a-lot was intact with only a small gouge in one cam lobe and an elongation of the cable loop.

The figure-8 knot was deformed, but intact, and it was possible to untie it with some effort.

Huff does not remember the accident or rappelling to the first belay ledge. When he arrived at the ledge, he was oriented only to his person and he did not know where he was, what had happened, or what day it was. Slowly he recovered these memories and an hour later he was fully aware and oriented, with the exception of the accident itself. (Source: E. Visnovske, Ranger, GTNP)

FALL ON ROCK, FAILURE TO FOLLOW ROUTE, NO EQUIPMENT, INADEQUATE CLOTHING, INEXPERIENCE
Wyoming, Grand Teton National Park, Mount Teewinot
On September 22, about 1300, Jon Winiasz (23) and Eliot Kalmbach (24)

were attempting to climb Mount Teewinot via the East Face route. They became severely off route and found themselves in technical terrain. They were unroped and had no climbing equipment. At approximately 11,600 feet, near the southeast ridge of the mountain, Kalmbach slipped and fell approximately 300 feet. He died on scene as a result of injuries received during the fall. Winiasz and the body of Kalmbach were evacuated by rangers using helicopter short-haul technique.

Analysis

Based on my interview with Winiasz, I determined that he was the more technical climber. He reported that he could climb 5.10 in the gym and some sport routes (bolted). He had climbed several third and fourth-class "14'ers" in Colorado and he had been rock climbing for two or three years. He described Kalmbach as having climbed in more places than he had, including Patagonia and Russia; however, he said Kalmbach was not much of a technical climber and most of his experience was in "scrambling". He indicated that his partner did not have a climbing harness or climbing shoes on this trip (and possibly did not own that type of equipment at all.) I found no technical climbing equipment during my inventory.

Winiasz stated that at one point during the climb, they went through a "hard section." Afterwards, the two had a discussion about turning around. Kalmbach told Winiasz that if they came to other spot like that, he would like to turn around. The immediate terrain above this point seemed reasonable so they continued on.

At the actual scene, the terrain changed very quickly from third-class (walking in loose rocks), to fourth-class (scrambling where you must use your hands), to fifth-class (generally climbed with a belay rope and special equipment and where a fall may result in injury or death). It is a spot very typical in the Tetons where the terrain is constantly changing back and forth from the relatively benign to the extreme.

Ultimately, these men found themselves in terrain that they were not prepared for, both in equipment and skills. There were several decisions, as well as several contributing factors, that were made on that day that led up to the accident:

Their decision to not back track when they realized that they were no longer on the Apex trail led them far from the East Face and the established route. Possibly their success on the Middle Teton the day before bolstered their confidence about staying on route and as a result, they may have underestimated the difficulty of Teewinot and the range in general. Staying on the trail most likely would have kept them on the East Face route; however, very technical terrain would still have been encountered and a similar accident could have happened on that route too.

Failing to recognize the severity of a fall from steep terrain may have changed things as well. From their discussion about turning around, they seemed to be aware that they were pushing the limits of their skills; however often the idea of falling and the resulting consequences seems remote when in fact it can happen almost anywhere at anytime in fifth-class terrain.

Based on their equipment, they seemed to be only partially prepared for the terrain they were in. I would estimate the difficulty from where the fall occurred in the 5.6 to 5.8 range. Most climbers would only venture into such terrain with a climbing harness, helmet, shoes, ropes, and protection. Additionally, most climbers venturing into the high peaks avoid cotton clothing and wear primarily synthetic materials. "Approach shoes" with a sticky rubber sole would be the standard for this type of climb, then switching to actual climbing shoes for the fifth-class portion. Kalmbach was wearing jeans and a t-shirt and standard hiking boots. (Source: E. Visnovske, Ranger, GTNP)

STATISTICAL TABLES

TABLE I
REPORTED MOUNTAINEERING ACCIDENTS

	Number of Accidents Reported		Total Persons Involved		Injured		Fatalities	
	USA	CAN	USA	CAN	USA	CAN	USA	CAN
1951	15		22		11		3	
1952	31		35		17		13	
1953	24		27		12		12	
1954	31		41		31		8	
1955	34		39		28		6	
1956	46		72		54		13	
1957	45		53		28		18	
1958	32		39		23		11	
1959	42	2	56	2	31	0	19	2
1960	47	4	64	12	37	8	19	4
1961	49	9	61	14	45	10	14	4
1962	71	1	90	1	64	0	19	1
1963	68	11	79	12	47	10	19	2
1964	53	11	65	16	44	10	14	3
1965	72	0	90	0	59	0	21	0
1966	67	7	80	9	52	6	16	3
1967	74	10	110	14	63	7	33	5
1968	70	13	87	19	43	12	27	5
1969	94	11	125	17	66	9	29	2
1970	129	11	174	11	88	5	15	5
1971	110	17	138	29	76	11	31	7
1972	141	29	184	42	98	17	49	13
1973	108	6	131	6	85	4	36	2
1974	96	7	177	50	75	1	26	5
1975	78	7	158	22	66	8	19	2
1976	137	16	303	31	210	9	53	6
1977	121	30	277	49	106	21	32	11
1978	118	17	221	19	85	6	42	10
1979	100	36	137	54	83	17	40	19
1980	191	29	295	85	124	26	33	8
1981	97	43	223	119	80	39	39	6
1982	140	48	305	126	120	43	24	14
1983	187	29	442	76	169	26	37	7
1984	182	26	459	63	174	15	26	6
1985	195	27	403	62	190	22	17	3
1986	203	31	406	80	182	25	37	14

	Number of Accidents Reported		Total Persons Involved		Injured		Fatalities	
	USA	CAN	USA	CAN	USA	CAN	USA	CAN
1987	192	25	377	79	140	23	32	9
1988	156	18	288	44	155	18	24	4
1989	141	18	272	36	124	11	17	9
1990	136	25	245	50	125	24	24	4
1991	169	20	302	66	147	11	18	6
1992	175	17	351	45	144	11	43	6
1993	132	27	274	50	121	17	21	1
1994	158	25	335	58	131	25	27	5
1995	168	24	353	50	134	18	37	7
1996	139	28	261	59	100	16	31	6
1997	158	35	323	87	148	24	31	13
1998	138	24	281	55	138	18	20	1
1999	123	29	248	69	91	20	17	10
2000	150	23	301	36	121	23	24	7
2001	150	22	276	47	138	14	16	2
2002	139	27	295	29	105	23	34	6
2003	118	29	231	32	105	22	18	6
2004	160	35	311	30	140	16	35	14
2005	111	19	176	41	85	14	34	7
2006	109		227		89		21	
2007	113		211		95		15	
2008	112		203		96		19	
2009	126		240		112		23	
Totals	6,571	958	11,979	2003	5,550	715	1,451	292

TABLE II

Geographical Districts	1951–2008			2009		
	Number of Accidents	Deaths	Total Persons Involved	Number of Accidents	Deaths	Total Persons Involved
CANADA*						
Alberta	520	142	1033			
British Columbia	317	119	641			
Yukon Territory	37	28	77			
New Brunswick	1	0	0			
Ontario	37	9	67			
Quebec	31	10	63			
East Arctic	8	2	21			
West Arctic	2	2	2			
Practice Cliffs[1]	20	2	36			
UNITED STATES						
Alaska	526	192	889	16	5	30
Arizona, Nevada						
Texas	95	18	172	2	0	5
Atlantic–North	1004	150	1733	22	0	30
Atlantic–South	118	27	207	5	1	10
California	1305	295	2585	26	3	52
Central	136	18	219	0	0	0
Colorado	779	216	2333	21	3	45
Montana, Idaho,						
South Dakota	84	33	135	2	2	5
Oregon	211	112	481	7	4	13
Utah, New Mexico	175	60	322	6	0	10
Washington	1050	321	898	12	3	27
Wyoming	569	133	1026	7	2	17

*No data from 2006–2009

[1]This category includes bouldering, artificial climbing walls, buildings, and so forth. These are also added to the count of each province, but not to the total count, though that error has been made in previous years. The Practice Cliffs category has been removed from the U.S. data.

TABLE III

	1951–08 USA	1959–04 CAN.	2009 USA	2009 CAN.
Terrain				
Rock	4530	528	77	
Snow	2367	355	41	
Ice	270	15	8	
River	15	3	0	
Unknown	22	10	0	
Ascent or Descent				
Ascent	3589	587	79	
Descent	1023	371	45	
Unknown	250	13	1	
Other[N.B.]	7	0	2	
Immediate Cause				
Fall or slip on rock	3589	290	59	
Slip on snow or ice	1023	207	27	
Falling rock, ice, or object	626	137	10	
Exceeding abilities	550	32	5	
Illness[1]	400	26	9	
Stranded	345	53	6	
Avalanche	294	127	5	
Rappel Failure/Error[2]	297	47	6	
Exposure	275	14	3	
Loss of control/glissade	211	17	4	
Nut/chock pulled out	236	9	7	
Failure to follow route	188	30	25	
Fall into crevasse/moat	165	50	2	
Faulty use of crampons	109	6	6	
Piton/ice screw pulled out	95	13	0	
Ascending too fast	66	0	1	
Skiing[3]	56	11	2	
Lightning	46	7	0	
Equipment failure	15	3	1	
Other[4]	491	37	31	
Unknown	61	10	0	
Contributory Causes				
Climbing unroped	1013	165	8	
Exceeding abilities	915	202	2	
Placed no/inadequate protection	762	96	32	
Inadequate equipment/clothing	690	70	11	
Weather	479	67	2	
Climbing alone	404	69	4	
No hard hat	348	71	6	

	1951–08 USA	1959–04 CAN	2009 USA	2009 CAN
Contributory Causes				
Inadequate belay	218	28	10	
Nut/chock pulled out	201	32	0	
Poor position	185	20	3	
Darkness	146	21	4	
Party separated	117	12	0	
Failure to test holds	101	32	4	
Piton/ice screw pulled out	86	13	0	
Failed to follow directions	73	12	0	
Exposure	64	16	0	
Illness[1]	40	9	0	
Equipment failure	11	7	0	
Other[4]	268	100	3	
Age of Individuals				
Under 15	1246	12	0	
15-20	1281	203	7	
21-25	1420	257	19	
26-30	1303	211	24	
31-35	1093	114	13	
36-50	1267	143	40	
Over 50	270	31	14	
Unknown	2002	530	27	
Experience Level				
None/Little	1777	304	8	
Moderate (1 to 3 years)	1635	354	15	
Experienced	2039	440	60	
Unknown	2083	559	55	
Month of Year				
January	235	25	6	
February	210	55	3	
March	315	68	6	
April	410	39	11	
May	938	62	19	
June	1081	70	19	
July	1154	254	20	
August	1057	184	18	
September	1184	75	7	
October	466	42	8	
November	199	20	4	
December	100	24	5	
Unknown	17	1	0	

	1951–08 USA	1959–04 CAN	2009 USA	2009 CAN
Type of Injury/Illness (Data since 1984)				
Fracture	1303	223	49	
Laceration	720	71	17	
Abrasion	348	76	13	
Bruise	496	83	16	
Sprain/strain	372	33	13	
Concussion	257	28	9	
Hypothermia	160	16	2	
Frostbite	132	12	2	
Dislocation	125	16	12	
Puncture	45	13	7	
Acute Mountain Sickness	45	0	0	
HAPE	73	0	1	
HACE	25	0	0	
Other[5]	331	49	19	
None	248	188	17	

N.B. Some accidents happen when climbers are at the top or bottom of a route, not climbing. They may be setting up a belay or rappel or are just not anchored when they fall. (This category created in 2001. The category "unknown" is primarily because of solo climbers.)

[1]These illnesses/injuries, which led directly or indirectly to the accident, include: minor foot injury from tight boots; chest pain (1 infection and 1 blocked artery); extreme fatigue and low O_2 sat. level; lower leg injuries; hypothermia; heart attack; hand-burn (from belay rope); dehydration; dislocation/sprain/strain—so had to be lowered (3).

[2]These included: rope diameter too small for Grigri; rope too short; no knot in end of rope; gear sling caught on rock—strangling climber.

[3]This category was set up originally for ski mountaineering. Backcountry touring or snow-shoeing incidents—even if one gets avalanched—are not in the data.

[4]These included: unable to self-arrest (8); failure to turn back (4); handhold/foothold came loose (4); ice came loose/gave away (2); ran out of food/water and no working stoves; misread snowpack; two bolt hangers "failed"; running rope through webbing—burned through; miscommunication (3); rappelling/lowering—rope too short (3), no knots in ends (3), rope diameter too small for Grigri; ice block came off (2); rappel rope stuck in crack; late start; fell on partner; dove on partner to stop fall; strangled in gear sling.

[5]These included: major chest pain (2); heart attack; extreme fatigue/low O_2 sat.; dehydration; hand burned by belay rope.

(Editor's Note: Under the category "other," many of the particular items will have been recorded under a general category. For example, the climber who dislodges a rock that falls on another climber would be coded as Falling Rock/Object. A climber who has a hand or foot-hold come loose and falls would be coded as Fall On Rock and Other—and most often includes Failure To Test Holds.)

MOUNTAIN RESCUE UNITS IN NORTH AMERICA
**Denotes team fully certified—Technical Rock,
Snow & Ice, Wilderness Search;
S, R, SI = certified partially in Search, Rock, and/or Snow & Ice

ALASKA
Alaska Mountain Rescue Group. PO Box 241102, Anchorage,
AK 99524. www.amrg.org
Denali National Park SAR. PO Box 588, Talkeetna, AK 99676.
Dena_talkeetna@nps.gov
Juneau Mountain Rescue, Inc. 2970 Foster Ave., Juneau, AK 99801
Sitka Mountain Search and Rescue. 209 Lake St., Sitka, AK 99835
US Army Alaskan Warfare Training Center. #2900 501 Second St., APO AP 96508

ARIZONA
Apache Rescue Team. PO Box 100, St. Johns, AZ 85936
Arizona Department Of Public Safety Air Rescue. Phoenix, Flagstaff, Tucson,
Kingman, AZ
Arizona Division Of Emergency Services. Phoenix, AZ
Grand Canyon National Park Rescue Team. PO Box 129, Grand Canyon, AZ 86023
**Central Arizona Mountain Rescue Team/Maricopa County Sheriff's Office
MR.** PO Box 4004 Phoenix, AZ 85030. www.mcsomr.org
Sedona Fire District Special Operations Rescue Team. 2860 Southwest Dr.,
Sedona, AZ 86336. ropes@sedona.net
**Southern Arizona Rescue Assn/Pima County Sheriff's Office. PO Box 12892,
Tucson, AZ 85732. http://hambox.theriver.com/sarci/sara01.html

CALIFORNIA
Altadena Mountain Rescue Team. 780 E. Altadena Dr., Altadena, CA 91001
www.altadenasheriffs.org/rescue/amrt.html
Bay Area Mountain Rescue Team. PO Box 19184, Stanford, CA 94309 bamru@
hooked.net
California Office of Emergency Services. 2800 Meadowview Rd., Sacramento, CA.
95832. warning.center@oes.ca.gov
China Lake Mountain Rescue Group. PO Box 2037, Ridgecrest, CA 93556
www.clmrg.org
Inyo County Sheriff's Posse SAR. PO Box 982, Bishop, CA 93514
inyocosar@juno.com
Joshua Tree National Park SAR. 74485 National Monument Drive,
Twenty Nine Palms, CA 92277. patrick_suddath@nps.gov
Malibu Mountain Rescue Team. PO Box 222, Malibu, CA 90265.
www.mmrt.org
Montrose SAR Team. PO Box 404, Montrose, CA 91021
Riverside Mountain Rescue Unit. PO Box 5444, Riverside,
CA 92517. www.rmru.org   rmru@bigfoot.com
San Bernardino County Sheriff's Cave Rescue Team. 655 E. Third St.
San Bernardino, CA 92415
www.sbsd-vfu.org/units/SAR/SAR203/sar203_1.htm

San Bernardino County So/ West Valley SAR. 13843 Peyton Dr., Chino Hills, CA 91709.

San Diego Mountain Rescue Team. PO Box 81602, San Diego, CA 92138. www.sdmrt.org

San Dimas Mountain Rescue Team. PO Box 35, San Dimas, CA 91773

Santa Barbara SAR Team. PO Box 6602, Santa Barbara, CA 93160-6602

Santa Clarita Valley SAR / L.A.S.O. 23740 Magic Mountain Parkway, Valencia, CA 91355. http://members.tripod.com/scvrescue/

Sequoia-Kings Canyon National Park Rescue Team. Three Rivers, CA 93271

Sierra Madre SAR. PO Box 24, Sierra Madre, CA 91025. www.mra.org/smsrt.html

Ventura County SAR. 2101 E. Olson Rd, Thousand Oaks, CA 91362 www.vcsar.org

Yosemite National Park Rescue Team. PO Box 577-SAR, Yosemite National Park, CA 95389

COLORADO

Alpine Rescue Team. PO Box 934, Evergreen, CO 80437 www.alpinerescueteam.org

Colorado Ground SAR. 2391 Ash St, Denver, CO 80222 www.coloradowingcap.org/CGSART/Default.htm

Crested Butte SAR. PO Box 485, Crested Butte, CO 81224

Douglas County Search And Rescue. PO Box 1102, Castle Rock, CO 80104. www.dcsarco.org info@dcsarco.org

El Paso County SAR. 3950 Interpark Dr, Colorado Springs, CO 80907-9028. www.epcsar.org

Eldorado Canyon State Park. PO Box B, Eldorado Springs, CO 80025

Grand County SAR. Box 172, Winter Park, CO 80482

Larimer County SAR. 1303 N. Shields St., Fort Collins, CO 80524. www.fortnet. org/LCSAR/ lcsar@co.larimer.co.us

Mountain Rescue Aspen. 630 W. Main St, Aspen, CO 81611 www.mountainrescueaspen.org

Park County SAR, CO. PO Box 721, Fairplay, CO 80440

Rocky Mountain National Park Rescue Team. Estes Park, CO 80517

Rocky Mountain Rescue Group. PO Box Y, Boulder, CO 80306 www.colorado.edu/StudentGroups/rmrg/ rmrg@colorado.edu

Routt County SAR. PO Box 772837, Steamboat Springs, CO 80477 RCSAR@co.routt.co.us

Summit County Rescue Group. PO Box 1794, Breckenridge, CO 80424

Vail Mountain Rescue Group. PO Box 1597, Vail, CO 81658 http://sites.netscape.net/vailmra/homepage vmrg@vail.net

Western State College Mountain Rescue Team. Western State College Union, Gunnison, CO 81231. org_mrt@western.edu

IDAHO

Bonneville County SAR. 605 N. Capital Ave, Idaho Falls, ID 83402 www.srv.net/~jrcase/bcsar.html

Idaho Mountain SAR. PO Box 741, Boise, ID 83701. www.imsaru.org rsksearch@aol.com

MAINE
Acadia National Park SAR. Bar Harbor, Maine

MARYLAND
**Maryland Sar Group. 5434 Vantage Point Road, Columbia, MD 21044
Peter_McCabe@Ed.gov

MONTANA
Glacier National Park SAR. PO Box 128, Glacier National Park,
West Glacier, MT 59936

Flathead County Search and Rescue. 920 South Main St., Kalispell, MT 59901.
Sheriff's Office phone: 406-758-5585.

NEVADA
**Las Vegas Metro PD SAR. 4810 Las Vegas Blvd., South Las Vegas,
NV 89119. www.lvmpdsar.com

NEW MEXICO
**Albuquerque Mountain Rescue Council. PO Box 53396, Albuquerque,
NM 87153. www.abq.com/amrc/ albrescu@swcp.com

NEW HAMPSHIRE
Appalachian Mountain Club. Pinkham Notch Camp, Gorham, NH 03581
Mountain Rescue Service. PO Box 494, North Conway, NH 03860

NEW YORK
76 SAR. 243 Old Quarry Rd., Feura Bush, NY 12067
Mohonk Preserve Rangers. PO Box 715, New Paltz, NY 12561
NY State Forest Rangers. 50 Wolf Rd., Room 440C, Albany, NY 12233

OREGON
**Corvallis Mountain Rescue Unit. PO Box 116, Corvallis, OR 97339
www.cmrv.peak.org

(S, R) Deschutes County SAR. 63333 West Highway 20, Bend, OR 97701

**Eugene Mountain Rescue. PO Box 20, Eugene, OR 97440

**Hood River Crag Rats Rescue Team. 2880 Thomsen Rd., Hood River,
OR 97031

**Portland Mountain Rescue. PO Box 5391, Portland, OR 97228
www.pmru.org info@pmru.org

PENNSYLVANNIA
**Allegheny Mountain Rescue Group. c/o Mercy Hospital,
1400 Locust, Pittsburgh, PA 15219. www.asrc.net/amrg

**Wilderness Emergency Strike Team. 11 North Duke Street, Lancaster,
PA 17602. www.west610.org

UTAH
**Davis County Sheriff's SAR. PO Box 800, Farmington, UT 84025. www.dcsar.org
Rocky Mountain Rescue Dogs. 3353 S. Main #122, Salt Lake City, UT 84115

Salt Lake County Sheriff's SAR. 3510 South 700 West, Salt Lake City, UT 84119
San Juan County Emergency Services. PO Box 9, Monticello, UT 84539
Utah County Sherrif's SAR. PO Box 330, Provo, UT 84603.
ucsar@utah.uswest.net
Weber County Sheriff's Mountain Rescue. 745 Nancy Dr, Ogden,
UT 84403. http://planet.weber.edu/mru
Zion National Park SAR. Springdale, UT 84767

VERMONT
Stowe Mountain Rescue. P.O. Box 291, Stowe, VT 05672. www.stowevt.org/htt/

VIRGINIA
Air Force Rescue Coordination Center. Suite 101, 205 Dodd Building,
Langley AFB, VA 23665. www2.acc.af.mil/afrcc/airforce.rescue@usa.net

WASHINGTON STATE
Bellingham Mountain Rescue Council. PO Box 292, Bellingham, WA 98225
Central Washington Mountain Rescue Council. PO Box 2663, Yakima, WA
98907. www.nwinfo.net/~cwmr/ cwmr@nwinfo.net
Everett Mountain Rescue Unit, Inc. 5506 Old Machias Road, Snohomish, WA
98290-5574. emrui@aol.com
Mount Rainier National Park Rescue Team. Longmire, WA 98397
North Cascades National Park Rescue Team. 728 Ranger Station Rd,
Marblemount, WA 98267
Olympic Mountain Rescue. PO Box 4244, Bremerton, WA 98312
www.olympicmountainrescue.org information@olympicmountainrescue.org
Olympic National Park Rescue Team. 600 Park Ave, Port Angeles, WA 98362
Seattle Mountain Rescue. PO Box 67, Seattle, WA 98111
www.eskimo.com/~pc22/SMR/smr.html
Skagit Mountain Rescue. PO Box 2, Mt. Vernon, WA 98273
Tacoma Mountain Rescue. PO Box 696, Tacoma, WA 98401
www.tmru.org
North Country Volcano Rescue Team. 404 S. Parcel Ave, Yacolt, WA 98675
www.northcountryems.org/vrt/index.html

WASHINGTON, DC
National Park Service, EMS/SAR Division. Washington, DC
US Park Police Aviation. Washington, DC

WYOMING
Grand Teton National Park Rescue Team. PO Box 67, Moose, WY 83012
Park County SAR, WY. Park County SO, 1131 11th, Cody, WY 82412

CANADA
North Shore Rescue Team. 147 E. 14th St, North Vancouver, B.C.,
Canada V7L 2N4
Rocky Mountain House SAR. Box 1888, Rocky Mountain House, Alberta,
Canada T0M 1T0

MOUNTAIN RESCUE ASSOCIATION
PO Box 880868
San Diego, CA 92168-0868
www.mra.org

Charley Shimanski, President
Alpine Rescue Team CO
67 Pauls Road, Evergreen, CO 80439
president@mra.org
303-832-5710 (w)   303-909-9348 (cell)
Term Expires June 2010

Neil Van Dyke, Vice President
Stowe Mountain Rescue, VT
PO Box 291, Stowe, VT 05672
vp@mra.org
802-253-9060
Term Expires June 2010

John Chang, Secretary/Treasurer
Bay Area Mountain Rescue
PO Box 19184, Stanford, CA 94309
sectreas@mra.org
925-699-2506 (cell)
Term Expires 2011

Doug Wessen, Member-at-Large
Juneau Mountain Rescue, Inc., AK
2970 Foster Ave., Juneau, AK 99801
dougwessen@gmail.com
907-586-4834
Term Expires 2010

Jim Frank, Member-at-Large
Santa Barbara SAR Team
PO Box 6602, Santa Barbara, CA 93160
j.frank@impulse.net
805-961-1621 (w)   805-452-3261 (cell)
Term Expires 2011

Kayley Trujillo, Executive Secretary
PO Box 880868, San Diego, CA 92168
info@mra.org
858-229-4295 (h)   951-317-5635 (cell)